THE STUDY OF LITERATURE

THE STUDY
OF
LITERATURE

AN EXISTENTIAL APPRAISAL

by

DAVIS DUNBAR McELROY

PHILOSOPHICAL LIBRARY

New York

70-661

To take things as they are,
Play with the cards one has,
Require one to be what one is.

—Gide, "Autumn Leaves"

CONTENTS

PREFACE

In a recent book, *Existentialism and Modern Literature* (Philosophical Library, 1963), I looked at modern literature from an existentialistic point of view. In this new book I have turned my attention to education in general and to the teaching of literature in particular.

In the first part, "Factories of the Mind," I attack American education for its infatuation with the intellect, for its neglect of all other human faculties, for its maniac insistence on viewing everything in creation with a machine-like objectivity, for its assembly-line methodology, and for its depersonalizing effect on everyone involved in it.

In the second part, "The Study of Literature," I have tried to show how the teaching of literature can be made more human. Some readers may feel that the book falls short in that it offers no definite scheme for improving present methods of teaching literature. I do not believe that the cure for what ails American education lies in changes in method, but in a shift of emphasis and a change in spirit. Almost any method will serve as long as students want to learn, teachers are willing to teach, and both remain human.

Basically what is wrong with education today is that it doesn't educate. As greater and greater emphasis is given to research over teaching, it becomes increasingly obvious that American education is geared to the accumulation of new knowledge. The present university set-up is perfect for this purpose, but much of value has been lost. For one thing we are calmly sacrificing the minds, souls, and bodies of millions of students to the building of a new Tower of Babel. As in the Bible story, we have reached the point where it seems to us that "nothing will be restrained from us which we have imagined to do." But, alas, it is also true that we have been confounded in our language.

When specialists in the same department no longer understand one another it is clear that we have been visited by a confusion of tongues. Specialists in the humanities have added as much to the confusion as anyone. Their claim that humanistic studies offer an escape from the dehumanizing effects of specialization is void. Other means must be found. It is my purpose in this book to suggest such means.

I have one debt of gratitude to pay before I begin. Of all the men I have known, Peter John Rempel of Washington State University stands out in the degree to which he embodies many of the human qualities I value most deeply. He is a living example of what intellect and learning can and should do for a man, in contrast to what they usually do. Knowing him has been the greatest encouragement to me in writing this book.

D. D. McE.

THE STUDY OF LITERATURE

PART I

FACTORIES OF THE MIND

CHAPTER I

EDUCATION FOR DESPAIR

The subject of Kierkegaard's small book, *The Sickness Unto Death*, is despair. But Kierkegaard's despair is not the emotion we know as despair, it is a state of being. When Kierkegaard says that a man is in "despair," he means that he does not have the courage to be himself. This must seem of small importance to most people, but to Kierkegaard it is man's fundamental psychological, ethical, and religious problem. Despair, he maintains, is "the sickness unto death," and he claims that to be healed of this sickness is a man's highest bliss. According to Kierkegaard, only six or seven men in each generation (he did not include himself in this number) escape despair.

If Kierkegaard is right, that everyone is sick unto death with despair, isn't it curious that so few of us are aware of it? Here is his answer: "A man in despair may nevertheless be perfectly well able to live on, to be a man, as it seems, occupy himself with temporal things, get married, beget children, win honor and esteem — and perhaps no one notices that in a deeper sense he lacks a self. About such a thing as that not much fuss is made in the world; for a self is the thing the world is least apt to inquire about, and the thing of all things the most dangerous for a man to let people notice that he has. The greatest danger, that of losing one's own self, may pass off as quietly as if it were nothing; every other loss, that of an arm, a leg, five dollars, a wife, etc., is sure to be noticed."

"By becoming wise about how things go in this world," he writes in another place, "a man in despair forgets himself, forgets what his name is (in the divine understanding of it), does not dare to believe in himself, finds it too venturesome a thing to be himself, far easier and safer to be like the others, to become an imitation, a number, a cipher in the crowd. This form of despair is hardly ever noticed in the world. Such a man, precisely by losing his self in this way, has gained perfectibility in adjusting himself to business, in making a success in the world. So far from being considered in despair, he is just what a man ought to be. He may be praised by men, be honored and esteemed, and pursue all the aims of temporal life. What is called worldliness is made up of just such men, who pawn themselves to the world. They use their talents, accumulate money, carry on worldly affairs, calculate shrewdly, are perhaps mentioned in history, but themselves they are not. Spiritually understood, they have no self, no self for whose sake they could venture everything — however selfish they may be for all that."

Such a man, it seems to me, is making a tragic mistake. Where he goes wrong is in assuming that all he is giving up is the personal satisfaction of being true to himself; he cannot believe that his temporizing way of life is costing him more than this. He is wrong. The neglected self does not die; it hovers about like an accusing phantom reminding him of what he could be if he chose. As a result he often suffers from guilt and anxiety which have no apparent cause. To escape his uneasiness he either becomes ceaselessly active in business or a profession, in politics or society; or he drugs himself with dope, drink, sex, gambling, or sports, anything that will enable him to escape his despair.

In *The Sickness Unto Death* Kierkegaard gives us a philosophical and psychological description of a man in despair. But his book is tough reading. Perhaps many readers will gain just as much from *The Trial,* a novel in which Franz Kafka portrays a man sick unto death with despair. The hero of this story, Joseph K, suffers anxiety, dread, and hopelessness, all of the spiritual sickness which Kierkegaard attributes to the man who is in "despair at not willing to be himself; or, still more serious, in despair at not willing to be a self at all."

Such men, as Kierkegaard says, get along very well in life; in fact they get along all the better for their despair. For them, as for Joseph K, their worldliness compensates for their utter spiritlessness, a state which Kierkegaard calls "Philistinism." A Philistine, Kierkegaard maintains, is forced to deny every possibility of a return of spirit, because if he admitted the possibility his Philistinism would be denying itself. Philistinism can make this denial because it thinks it is in control of possibility; it believes that "it carries possibility around like a prisoner in the cage of the probable, shows it off, imagines itself to be the master." What Philistinism fails to notice is that in doing this "it has taken itself captive to be the slave of spiritlessness and to be the most pitiful of all things." Because Philistinism betrays a man in this way, Kierkegaard says, the worldly man can never become conscious of his despair. But he does not escape it; on the contrary, "his unknowing," Kierkegaard says, has the effect of "putting him under arrest to himself." This is Joseph K's situation exactly.

The most frightening thing about Kafka's K is that he is exactly like me. When his unexpected "arrest" forces him to examine his past life "down to the smallest actions and accidents," he complains bitterly against such a "dreary task." "It would do well enough as an occupation for one's second childhood in years of retirement, when the long days needed filling up. But at this time when he should be devoting his mind entirely to work, when every hour was hurried and crowded — for he was still in full career and rapidly becoming a rival even to the Deputy Manager of the bank where he worked — when his evenings and nights were all too short for the pleasures of a bachelor life, this was the time when he must sit down to such a task!" Plainly K was so busy making a living and enjoying himself that he did not give himself a chance to live. The same can be said about me.

It is the bitterest irony that K's empty and meaningless life of worldly striving and pleasure is precisely the kind of life we regard as "really living." The true value of such a life is revealed at the end of the book when K is executed by two brutal assassins because he can find no reason why he should be allowed to go on merely existing. Before his death, however, K finally realizes that while he was "snatching at the world with twenty hands, and not for a very laudable motive either," he had thrown away his life.

Although there are a number of things about *The Trial* I do not understand, the main point of the story is clear to me. The only way that K could have saved himself would have been by daring to be himself, to be "an individual man, this definite individual man, alone in this tremendous exertion and this tremendous responsibility," as Kierkegaard says. It is precisely because K hasn't the strength or the will to be himself that he is "accused of guilt," tried, condemned, and executed. Through the story of K's trial and death, Kafka shows us what it really means to live in despair, to be sick unto death with the triviality and meaninglessness of one's life.

The Trial is not the only work of literature to portray a man in despair. Walker Percy, in a recent novel he calls *The Moviegoer,* leans heavily on Kierkegaard. How do I know? Well for one thing he quotes Kierkegaard in a epigraph: "The specific character of despair is precisely this, it is unaware of being despair." That's from *The Sickness Unto Death.* What's more important, his hero, Binx Bolling, is engaged in an unremitting struggle with malaise, the sick boredom of an empty and meaningless existence. Bolling is very good at making money. "Our name is increase," he says exultantly when he learns that he stands to make a cool fifteen thousand on a piece of property. But in the end he finds he cannot stand a life of mere moneymaking and casual love affairs. He gives up his business career to go in for medical research and marriage.

In a darker study of despair, *The Death of a Salesman,* Arthur Miller shows how the doctrine of success at any price can kill. Like most Americans, the hero of this drama, Willy Loman, worships popularity, power, and money, even though he has none of these things. Like most Americans Loman has none of the spiritual resources which depend upon a man being his true self. When he loses his job he discovers that all he is actually worth is his life insurance. To cash in on this he kills himself. Loman wants the money to go to his oldest son, so that the son, at least, can live up to his father's shoddy dreams of success.

6

Walker Percy's hero survives his ordeal of despair, Arthur Miller's succumbs. The decisive difference between them is that Binx Bolling, the moviegoer, accepts responsibility for the future; Willy Loman doesn't. Loman kills himself; Bolling changes his life. Few people today will accept responsibility for anything, let alone the future. It is no wonder Willy Loman's suicide upsets them.

Arthur Miller's play disturbs Americans deeply for other reasons as well. We all realize perfectly well that what happened to Willy could happen to any of us. Above all we dread the suffering and the pain of failure, and the play brings this dread to the surface. But Willy's failure was as a man, not a salesman; he killed himself because he was in despair, not because he lost his job. To a real person failure can be even more rewarding than success. Herman Melville believed (and demonstrated his belief in his own life) that a man *must* fail. If he settles for success, he always stops short of his greatest potentiality. Melville was willing to risk the sin and suffering of failure; most of us are not. It has been said of us that we do not believe in the necessity of sin and suffering, therefore we have no souls. I think there is something in this, as uncomfortable as it makes me feel. Anyway I am convinced that the person who can laugh it off is really in despair.

For the moment let us suppose that Kierkegaard is right that most of us are in despair; how did we get this way? The answer, I think, is that it has never been easy to be oneself, but many things in modern life now make it more difficult than ever, and education plays its part. To begin with, our lives have been impoverished by mass-production, no matter how cluttered up they have become with the things we produce. Anyone who does not share popular tastes, who is not satisfied with what everyone else wants, is penalized. He can get what he wants only at great expense. Similarly, anyone can dress and act differently from everyone else, but he must pay the price of loneliness. Thus an individual taste is a social as well as an economic handicap. The result is that nearly everyone is forced to live in a mass-produced way: we live in mass-produced houses, wear mass-produced clothes, and eat mass-produced foods. As Ernest Van den Haag puts it, "We are born in hospitals, fed in cafeterias, married in hotels; we die in hospitals, we rest briefly in funeral homes, and we are finally incinerated." Is it any wonder that so many who live and die like this become classless, rootless, cultureless, selfless automatons?

Perhaps mass production would not have had as great an effect on our lives were it not for advertising, which makes mass production possible by standardizing tastes. Some social critics have accused advertisers of deliberately manipulating our tastes to their economic advantage. This is good melodrama, but I think there is a better explanation.

I believe that advertisers are perfectly willing to advertise, and manufacturers to produce, anything whatsoever providing enough people will buy it. They have no desire to raise or lower the taste of consumers, but merely to find out what their taste is so that they can satisfy the greatest number. The end result of this process of producing the greatest amount of goods for the greatest number is the de-individualization of everything produced: cars, clothes, cosmetics, television entertainment, movies, beauty queens, homes, home furnishings — the list is endless. In an effort to overcome the vague dissatisfaction which most of us feel with mass-produced things, manufacturers try to "personalize" them by putting our initials on them. But this dodge only reveals how bleakly impersonal these things are.

In our schools, which have become department stores of ideas in which teachers wait on student customers who are shopping around for bargains in ideas, the same process of de-individualization is taking place. Van den Haag says that educators long ago recognized that "success is hindered by a discriminating personal taste which expresses an individual personality, and success is fostered by an unselective appetite." Convinced of this, American educators, like those in Huxley's *Brave New World*, "begin in nursery school to avoid elaboration of personal discernment and to instill fear of separation from the group. Group acceptance is stressed through formal and informal popularity contests, teamwork, and polling." By the time students reach college, they are afraid to open their minds and mouths for fear of saying or thinking something offensive to their "peer group." This explains in part the phenomenon of the so-called silent generation.

For the most part, higher education continues and confirms the results of this depersonalizing process. Higher education does this through the propagation of three doctrines, doctrines which lead inexorably to despair: the doctrine of the supremacy of the intellect, the doctrine of selfless objectivity, and the doctrine of success at any price.

The doctrine of success at any price is flamboyantly apparent in college sports. A great many educators must have come to the conclusion at one time or another that the rah-rah sports, especially football, are a confounded nuisance. Many still believe in sports, but they wince when such evils as crass professionalism and gambling corruption are brought up. A majority of students enjoy watching games, though an increasing number say they are indifferent. But even the indifferent students will argue the desirability and even the necessity of competitive sports in college. Somehow they manage to convey the impression that much more is involved than the honor and prestige of the school.

This bothered me for a long time. Then one day I was walking by a playing field where an ordinary physical education class was being put through its paces in one of the middle-distance runs, perhaps the 440. The students were started in groups of five, and at the end of the run the order in which they finished was recorded. "If they are being taught to run," I asked myself, "why must they compete?" Once those students finish college it is very unlikely they will ever run footraces again. The element of competition, therefore, must serve some other purpose. The thought occurred to me that this purpose must be to prepare students to succeed in the perpetual "footrace" of our competitive society. College sports, I concluded, serve to uphold the doctrine of success at any price by instilling the competitive spirit.

It is the alumni, notice, who are most cast down when the old school team has a losing streak. They also contribute most of the money to pay the players' salaries. I suspect that their despondency during a bad season has very little to do with the game, but a great deal to do with the mystique of worldly success. In the business world there is no such thing as playing the game for the sake of the game — the important thing is to come out on top. This is the kind of success that the doctrine of success at any price aims at, and this kind of success is worshipped at every stage in the educative process. And at every stage the same spirit reigns as on the football field. When colleges compete on the television in a quiz game it is no accident that the program is called "College Bowl."

What is wrong with competition? Nothing. Everything depends upon what you compete for. One person can compete with another in kindness, consideration, humility, tolerance, meekness, honesty, sincerity, but who does? The competition being fostered by the doctrine of success at any price is fatal to these things. In such competition, Brooks Adams observed, the flesh always prevails over the spirit. Americans, he says, have failed to rise above their servitude to the flesh. "On the contrary, our democracy deifies competition, preaching it as the highest destiny and true duty of man. Christ taught that we should love our enemies. To compete successfully the flesh decrees that we must kill them. And the flesh prevails."

Adams explains further that our belief that "it is possible by education to stimulate the selfish interest of competition, which demands that each man should strive to better himself at the cost of his neighbor, so as to coincide with the moral principle that all should labor for the common good" is a jarring contradiction. He is right. In order to compete, in order to succeed in our world, we must suppress our better selves, and this inevitably leads us to despair. On top of this the abrogation of self which enables a student to surrender himself to the doctrine of success at any price, as all of them do, is made absolute by the doctrine of the supremacy of the intellect and the doctrine of selfless objectivity.

I do not believe that there is one person in a thousand in the academic world who seriously questions the doctrine that education demands selfless objectivity from both teacher and student. Most people, in fact, have no notion that any other kind of education is possible. When Paul Tillich expresses his belief that "the way into the profounder levels of life is not to be found by means of science and psychology, but only by means of intuitive insight, of apprehension on the basis of one's own aliveness," most academics won't know what he is talking about.

Tillich complains that there is no place for this kind of learning because a capitalistic spirit dominates, a spirit which reduces education exclusively to a rational transaction between teacher and student. Kierkegaard, too, has some ideas about education which are less likely to be understood even than Tillich's. Kierkegaard insists that truth is "an objective uncertainty held fast in an appropriation process of the most passionate inwardness." He also believes that everything we learn should serve for our edification. He feels that "indifferent" learning — that is, learning approached with selfless objectivity — so far from being admirable, is "an inhuman sort of curiosity."

Where does American education stand from Kierkegaard's point of view? It must be obvious to everyone that it stands exactly nowhere. That which is "edifying" makes me a better person. Now I must stop and explain what I mean by "a better person." Apparently this is something we are not taught in school, or anywhere else for that matter. By a better person I mean kinder, more loving, tolerant, self-reliant, genuinely friendly, generous, open, things like that. Does our education help us to develop these qualities? Quite the contrary: it holds worldly success and power up as the highest goal as it busily prepares us for a lifetime of struggle in the jungle of our competitive world.

In our education all knowledge is treated as "indifferent"; the only value it has for us is as a means for success. In all our knowing we are encouraged to suppress the subjective self in favor of selfless objectivity. We believe we must remain detached, aloof, impersonal. So far from regarding knowledge as edifying, we are taught to manipulate facts and ideas as if they were things. This is not edification, it is education for despair.

The trouble is we have a false idea of objectivity. Erich Fromm explains that "objectivity is not, as it is often implied in a false idea of 'scientific' objectivity, synonymous with detachment, with absence of interest and care. *Objectivity does not mean detachment, it means respect;* that is, the ability not to distort and to falsify things, persons, and oneself. The idea that lack of personal interest is a condition for recognizing the truth is mistaken."

Let me give an example of what this false idea of objectivity leads to. On several occasions I have been asked to talk to students who are curious about existentialism. I usually begin by telling them a true thing, they go to too many lectures. If you really want to know what existentialism is all about, I tell them, go read some books by people who call themselves existentialists. Surprisingly enough nobody has ever walked out on me. Next I tell them that existentialism has provided me with a philosophy of life, something I can believe in. Their reactions are curious; most of them, I think, are actually embarrassed. I cannot think why. All I know is that the last thing they expected me to say was that I believed in existentialism.

I suspect that most of them haven't the slightest intention of ever taking up existentialism. They merely want to be informed about it, but it will always remain just another bit of information which they push around in their minds. Why they bother at all is more than I can figure out. Kierkegaard says that if we "know" a thing (as these students "know" about existentialism), and yet we go ahead and act as if we did not know it at all, then we do not know it in the true sense of knowing. I believe in existentialism because it offers me a way to escape from despair. As long as these students view existentialism with detachment it can never help them.

I know from past experience that my attack on the doctrine of selfless objectivity will strike many as completely wrongheaded. Well and good. But let me ask this question: Where in our depersonalized standards of thinking and writing is there a place for *me,* the thinker and writer? Everyone seems to assume that I have to wipe myself out of existence before I can say anything worth listening to. That's crazy. Many of my students express doubts when I advocate writing in the first person. They are convinced that you lose points whenever you say or write "I." This is more than student folklore: a leading physicist, P. W. Bridgman, expresses his belief that our standards of philosophical and scientific writing reveal an obsession with the ideal of a coldly impersonal generality. Bridgman regards this neglect of the thinker and writer as one of the fundamental difficulties in the way the human race handles its mind.

It is refreshing to hear this scientist reaffirm the subjectivity of all knowledge, and express his belief in the necessity of writing in the first person. Bridgman's insistence on the role of the thinker in science comes from his conviction that what proves something to me may not prove anything to you, and therefore "proof" is a very subjective affair which is of necessity private rather than public. The conviction that all knowledge is subjective led Bridgman to insist that "if immediate experience is to be communicated with any faithfulness or freshness, scientific reports must be written in the first person."

Now the curious thing is that humanists, who have long been critical of scientists for thinking and writing like machines, will have nothing to do with Bridgman's ideas. Humanists scoff at a truth which they ought never to have abandoned — that in all knowledge there is as much of the knower as of the known, as Spinoza said. Instead, they cling desperately to the ideal of selfless objectivity which they inherited from the kind of science which Bridgman, in the name of modern physics, repudiates. I am reminded of the story that long ago the Irish gave a bagpipe to the Scots, and that the Scots haven't caught on to the joke yet. Scientists long ago convinced humanists of the value of selfless objectivity, and the humanists still have not caught on that the trouble with objective thinking is that it turns everything it touches into an object. Now that modern science has returned to subjectivity, humanists are clinging grimly to their bagpipe of selfless objectivity.

Humanists are also clinging grimly to the doctrine of the supremacy of the intellect. Perhaps this explains how it has come about that the most pointed criticism of the way our minds work comes from scientists and not from humanists. In his *Creative Evolution*, Henri Bergson explains that our intellects feel at home only among inanimate objects, especially among solids, for our concepts have been formed on the model of solids and therefore our logic is the logic of solids. According to Bergson, this accounts for the fact that the intellect, "so skillful in dealing with the inert, is awkward the moment it touches the living. Whether it wants to treat the life of the body or the life of the mind, it proceeds with the rigor, the stiffness and the brutality of an instrument not designed for such use. We tend to think all reality, however fluid, under the form of the sharply defined solid. We are at ease only in the discontinuous, in the immobile, in the dead. *The intellect,*" Bergson concludes, *"is characterized by a natural inability to comprehend life."* Another Frenchman, Andre Gide, makes the same point a bit more imaginatively: "Trying to understand life with the intellect is like trying to grasp a flame with tongs." Both these men are convinced that what is wrong with the doctrine of the supremacy of the intellect is that it prevents us from understanding life.

The doctrine of the supremacy of the intellect has another drawback: it makes us think we understand everything. "The misfortune of the present age," says Kierkegaard, "is not that it is one-sided, but that it is abstractly all-sided. A one-sided person rejects, clearly and definitely, what he does not wish to include; but the abstractly all-sided person imagines that he has everything through the one-sidedness of the intellect."

My own conviction is this: I regard the intellect as man's most useful faculty. But this does not mean that it is man's only useful faculty, as the way we are educated would lead us to believe. We make too much of it, everything in fact; that is my objection. By turning ourselves over to our intellects we have seriously crippled or destroyed the richest part of ourselves, our emotions. When the intellect is put in charge, it is not content merely to be supreme, it wants to exclude everything else. Given the chance, it will suppress everything that is not itself, and it will suppress it absolutely if it can. This is what is happening to our emotions under the doctrine of the supremacy of the intellect.

"Happiness," writes Erich Fromm, "means being interested in life, responding to life not just with one's brain but with one's whole personality. In education, intellectual development is not enough. Education must be both intellectual *and* emotional. In modern society we find an increasing separation between intellect and feeling. The experiences of man today are mainly experiences of thought rather than an immediate grasp of what his heart feels, his eyes see, and his ears hear. In fact, this separation between intellect and feeling has led modern man to a near schizoid state of mind in which he has become almost incapable of experiencing anything except in thought."

Once again I know from past experience that anything I have to say about the limitations of the intellect is certain to be taken as an attack on reason itself. Heidegger had the same trouble: "Because I have spoken out against 'logic,' people conclude that I demand that the rigor of thinking be abandoned and that in its place the irrational arbitrariness of blind urges and emotions be enthroned. For what is more 'logical' than to assume that he who speaks out against 'logic' defends the irrational. What is going on here? With the aid of the much heralded logic and *ratio* they argue that what is not positive must of necessity be negative. And they are so filled to the brim with 'logic' that everything that runs counter to the customary drowsiness of thinking must be branded as a damnable negation."

Heidegger's complaint that every time he raises objections to current modes of thought he is accused of advocating the extreme opposite reveals once again the intolerance of the intellect. The modern mind, under the dominance of the intellect, habitually excludes the middle. Things have got to be either one hundred per cent one way, or one hundred per cent the other — nothing in between will serve. In attacking the doctrine of the supremacy of the intellect, I am bound to be understood as advocating that some other human faculty (the emotions, for example) must be made supreme. Will nothing less than this satisfy? Neither the intellect, nor the emotions, nor the body should be supreme; all human faculties should work in harmonious concord — that is what I am trying to put across in this book.

It's a wan hope, but I would like to see a revival of Goethe's concept of reason. Reason to Goethe was a man's inner nature or "self" which makes him what he is. To live according to reason, then, would be to become one's true self. Intellect, Goethe said, must be guided by reason, for intellect belongs to the practical realm; it does not extend into the realm of judgment. The intellect needs the guide of reason because if it is left to itself it produces anarchy. Thus to abandon man to his intellect is to deprive him of all sense of responsibility. This is why the doctrine of the supremacy of the intellect is causing, and will continue to cause, an incalculable amount of mischief. Goethe, who saw the unrestrained intellect at work in the science of his day, warned his generation that they were denying respect for human life. Today we see that this denial has become absolute. Through science the pure intellect has created weapons which could easily bring an end to the human race.

These weapons of absolute destruction, however, are only symptoms of something much deeper, much more dangerous, much more deadly. As Erich Fromm puts it: "We have lost the sense of the significance and uniqueness of the individual; we have made ourselves into instruments for purposes outside ourselves; we experience and treat ourselves as commodities; and our own powers have become alienated from ourselves. We have become things and our neighbours have become things. The result is that we feel powerless and despise ourselves for our impotence, and we have no conscience, since we do not trust our own judgment."

If this is true about us, and I believe that it is true, can there be any doubt that through the doctrines of despair which prevail in our schools we are leading the innocent to slaughter? In *The Decline of the West,* Oswald Spengler predicted that the supremacy of the intellect would have the direst consequences for our civilization. Spengler could be wrong, Fromm could be wrong, Goethe could be wrong, I could be wrong; I hope we are all wrong, as wrong as can be. But I am filled with the gravest apprehensions for the future when I see successive waves of college students meekly and submissively turning themselves over to our institutions of higher learning to be educated for despair.

CHAPTER II

LITERATURE AS AN OBJECT

Nowhere in education is the depersonalizing effect of the doctrines of the supremacy of the intellect and of selfless objectivity so apparent as in the teaching of literature. Perhaps that is why, being a teacher of literature, I am more aware of their effect than most teachers.

The purpose of the study of literature as it is laid down by English departments in school catalogs and elsewhere usually consists of some high-sounding flapdoodle about cultural attainments and the development of the whole man. Just why it is that cultural priority should be given to literature in a society which is scientific and technological before everything else is never made clear. Matthew Arnold's definition of culture as "all the best that is known and thought" has none of this exclusiveness. Furthermore, since teachers of literature are as highly specialized as anyone else, it is hard to see the justness of their self-appointed role of preventing others from becoming too one-sided.

Come to think of it, is there any real likelihood that specialists of any kind can turn out students less one-sided than themselves? In *The Great Gatsby*, F. Scott Fitzgerald refers to the well-rounded man as "that most limited of all specialists," and perhaps the most common criticism of the way literature is being taught seems to bear this out. Students complain that the professional specialists who teach literature insist on turning them into carbon copies of an English professor. Recently I heard of an engineer who says that what English teachers really mean when they talk about "well-roundedness," is "be more like me." He has a point.

If we ignore all the fine-sounding official propaganda and take a good look at the actual value placed on literature by those who teach it, we will discover that they regard it as an object among other objects. For the most part, literature is presented as objective subject matter which is to be mastered and manipulated in the same way as any other subject matter. For example, an attempt is made to give students a factual knowledge of literature so that they will have something tangible to take away with them. Students are also instructed, sometimes with surprising thoroughness, in techniques of interpretation, analysis, criticism, and the other ways in which literature can be manipulated.

What they are not taught is to take literature itself seriously — seriously enough, that is, to let it affect them deeply or permanently. The end they have in view may be to get by a college-board examination, to obtain a degree, to run up a few grade points, to turn themselves into English teachers — in short, anything but the serious study of literature for the purpose of edification; for the purpose, that is, of making themselves different, even better, than they are. Instead, they are easily "humbugged by the high aloofness of indifferent learning," as Kierkegaard puts it.

Students and teachers alike have absolutely no suspicion that literature offers a way "to venture wholly to be oneself, as an individual man, this definite individual man, alone in this tremendous exertion and this tremendous responsibility," which is Kierkegaard's criterion for all learning which is not mere jest and vanity. Indeed, if the suspicion ever entered their heads, they would immediately thrust literature aside, for it is characteristic of the modern temper to shun the exertion, the responsibility, and the fearful isolation of being differentiated from the mass.

Since I have raised so many objections, perhaps it would be well for me to set down what I hold to be the true aim of the study of literature. Like Matthew Arnold, I believe we study literature to find out who we are and how we ought to live. I assume that when a work of literature is meaningful to me, I must be somehow different than I was before I read it. This difference may be great or small, but it is essential. If a work of literature does not affect me in this way, if I merely enjoy it or use it as an object in any of the ways I have described, it has no real meaning for me as a person.

To the objection that this gives a student of literature too much license to ignore important and difficult books, I reply that surely it is a great waste to become concerned over books which do not move us, no matter how great they are thought to be. Goethe said that unless a book is read "from a certain one-sided enthusiasm, or from a loving interest in the person and the work, the result is hardly worth considering." It is only when you read a book, "and let it work on you, and yield yourself up entirely to its influence that you arrive at a correct judgment of it."

Two possible objections will be raised to Goethe's idea: one is that students of literature will stagnate at a level of reading beneath their full capacity; the other is that they will find all too few books to which they can give their sympathy, enthusiasm, and loving interest. I will not bother to answer these objections because I know very well that they do not express what is most offensive in Goethe's idea, its subjectivity. Goethe's meaning is unmistakable: if literary judgments are to be of any value, they must be subjective. I dare say that there are lots of teachers of literature who will agree with him. In my experience, however, a far greater number reveal a distrust of subjectivity in any form, and of emotional subjectivity most of all.

I find it very difficult to understand why it is that so many teachers of literature distrust emotion. The word "solipsistic" is forever on the tip of their tongues when an emotional response is suspected. Yet art works to a very considerable extent through the very emotions they repudiate. How good an understanding and appreciation of literature will students get if their emotional responses are suppressed or dismissed as irrelevant, uninteresting, distasteful, and undesirable?

I recall that once in an undergraduate examination I wrote that Shakespeare's Brutus would make a very uncomfortable friend.

19

Whoever read the examination put the word "rot" opposite my comment. For the moment my annoyance was disproportionate to the offense — I admit that. When I cooled down, however, this was replaced by curiosity: I began to wonder what was in the reader's mind. Since I cannot believe that anyone really wants the kind of friend who will stick a knife in you on principle, I can only assume that the fellow regarded my repugnance for this killing kind of friendship as out of order. He had been trained to regard such responses as uncritical. True criticism, to his mind, had to be impersonal, aloof, unimpassioned, and wholly objective. In other words it should have all the precision and rigidity of a science.

You can't talk to such people about the need for emotional subjectivity in the study of literature. Foremost in their minds is the fear that if students respond in this way they will wantonly misunderstand what they have read. I must admit that this is very distressing. Nevertheless I still believe that students must be allowed to work things out for themselves. We ought not to assume that they will go through life in ignorance unless we stuff them full of certified ideas and opinions. A student who is capable of an occasional good idea of his own, or of asking a good question, is certainly as well prepared as one whose head is jammed full of the best ideas that *we* give him, though he makes a multitude of errors. If students are to be permitted to use their own powers of understanding and judgment, the study of literature has got to be a pretty solipsistic affair. It is true that rigorous insistence on accepted objective standards will inhibit students from distorting what they read, but all too often this has the affect of immunizing them from responding to literature altogether.

To this I will add that in banishing emotional subjectivity from the study of literature, we have banished moral considerations as well; for emotions are an inseparable part of morality, and you cannot exclude one without excluding the other. The objective intellect is indifferent to right and wrong. Of course it must be understood that the idea of morality here ranges far beyond the narrow limits of sex, to which most people nowadays confine it. I am quite aware that most critics, scholars, and teachers are violently opposed to any suggestion that morality is an inescapable part of literature. I wish I could make them see that the study of literature lacks purpose whenever moral issues are excluded.

The present situation has its humorous side. In his little book on Matthew Arnold, *Poetry and the Criticism of Life,* H. W. Garrod points out that the reaction of many readers today to morality in literature is "to bury their heads in the bedclothes, seeking safety in form and expression until the ethical terror be overpast." Garrod asks, and rightly so, what on earth it is that they are so afraid of? For one thing, I would say, they are afraid of committing themselves. Moral issues in literature, unlike those in ethical systems and dogmatics, demand individual responses. Confronted with a moral issue in literature, the reader has to make an individual judgment which he is not prepared to make. The modern mind, trained to think "scientifically," feels all at sea once it is outside a system.

Jacob Burckhardt's general observation on the arts is applicable here: "The arts arise from mysterious vibrations communicated to the soul, and, just because they are not sciences, they have no laws to discover." In literature, as in life, we have to judge a particular moral issue, raised for a specific person, by a given set of circumstances — and from this individual judgment no abstraction, no generalization can be made. We cannot surrender our judgment to any existing ethical or moral code without going astray. Since literary criticism in the current mode reaches out for abstractions and generalizations, who can wonder that it shuns morality?

I will be more particular. Before we understand Hamlet, we must put ourselves in his place as completely as we can. This means that we must be capable of feeling as he felt as well as thinking his thoughts. We must feel the frustration and anguish of his dilemma, the impossible choice between two evils, the irresolution, the lethargy, the melancholy of being unable to choose. This is not, nor should it be, a matter of mere critical manipulation. Hamlet's problem is our problem too. As Lawrence Durrell says in *The Black Book,* "The modern disease looming in the world is the terrible disintegration of action under the hideous pressure of the ideal; the disease of a world every day more accurately portrayed by Hamlet."

As long as Hamlet's dilemma remains merely an intellectual puzzle we can study the play without the uncomfortable realization that it portrays our situation too. Most people, I think, would prefer not to face the play in this way. I am reminded of a student who once said in a discussion of Arthur Miller's *The Death of a Salesman*, that her boy-friend (who was studying business administration) said to her: "Listen, I don't want to talk about it; I don't want to think about it; I just want to forget it!" I expect many people will feel the same way about *Hamlet*, once they ask themselves whether we are going to be any better at solving our problems than Hamlet was.

For example, what are we to do with genocidal weapons we dare not use on others, yet cannot give up for fear others may use them on us? We have to face the fearful truth that there is no answer to this question — it is insoluble. When Hamlet faced up to his insoluble dilemma he lost the will to live. Are we any different? In such a situation the modern temper finds that the safest thing to do is to view things objectively; that is, to turn Shakespeare's play into an object. When the chips are down we back off from the demands that great literature makes of us.

Some such motive as this, I suspect, lies behind the attempt in the past fifty years or so to make the study of literature "scientific." Were this not so, there would be a much greater awareness that scientific thinking, which is indispensable when it comes to the manipulation of objects, kills when it is applied to literature. As Lewis Mumford points out, the inhuman and machinelike quality of scientific thought is suggested by the popular notion of the scientist: "cold, detached, rigorous, unemotional, in a word, *objective.*" All these words, Mumford says, are considered laudatory by the scientist.

Mumford then goes on to say that "science, by its method, disengages the scientist from life, from the real world and the real self in which emotions, imagination and dreams are as real as instrument measurement." He suggests that "in order to concentrate

22

effectively on his own limited object, the scientist has deliberately fabricated for himself a defective personality by suppressing his emotional and sexual nature." The pity is that most teachers of literature have done the same thing to themselves.

But this process of depersonalization and dehumanization does not stop with the scientist and the teacher of literature — it has influenced us all. This may account for the deep distrust we have of our emotions. In order to set our intellects free, we have all crippled ourselves emotionally and sexually, as Mumford says. Moreover, I am convinced that Bergson is right, that the intellect is at ease only when it is dealing with objects. This is why the intellectual approach to literature turns it into an object, a thing without life.

What is even worse, when we turn our intellects against ourselves we too become mere objects, things of no consequence in a world of things. This accounts for the fact that most people today regard their actions as insignificant once they range outside the tiny world of their personal affairs. They think of themselves in this inhuman way because their minds have been trained to think objectively about the greater world, and in no other way. The only possible way anyone can persuade himself that *he* matters is subjectively. in the face of the vast, indifferent forces at large in the world, the feeling or emotional conviction that *I* am important, and that what *I* do matters, is all that can give meaning to life. But it is almost impossible to feel this way about oneself in our world. In the face of a hundred megaton bomb, what do *I* matter? Less than a flyspeck.

There is another side to this, a side that most people do not like any more than the subjectivity they have repudiated. If what I do matters, then I am also responsible for everything I do, and for whatever happens to me as well. Jean-Paul Sartre insists that this responsibility goes as far back as my conception. Of course this is absurd, but that is not the reason people laugh it off. They do not relish this kind of responsibility at all; they want to feel that they are the *victims,* not the perpetrators, of the evil in the world.

Yet in a certain sense we are all guilty whenever an inhuman act is committed, as Dostoevsky teaches.

Dostoevsky's belief, like Sartre's, does not rest on logic, but on the conviction that unless you accept this kind of responsibility your life will never have the meaning in it that you long for. Most people cannot accept this responsibility because their intellects will not let them, because the proposition is absurd. Nevertheless the acceptance of total responsibility is the basic challenge of modern life. The tragedy is that most people dare not, or will not face it; therefore they condemn themselves to meaningless lives. Instead, they allow the novelty, the speed, and the comfort of modern living to lull them into a state of lethargic passivity. Perhaps this is what T. S. Eliot had in mind when he wrote that the world will end, "not with a bang but a whimper."

CHAPTER III

THE SPECIALIST AS "MASS-MAN"

To my mind Ortega y Gasset's *The Revolt of the Masses* is the most penetrating study of our present social and cultural situation that I have ever read. Therefore I find it very curious that no paperback edition has been available for the past six or seven years. A few years ago a friend of mine wrote the publisher who had once issued a paperback edition, urging him to reissue it. The publisher wrote back that there was no call for it. Recently this same publisher brought out a *new* paperback, which means the old plates were destroyed. I can only assume from this that at one time he was convinced there was no interest in the book. But there is something fishy about all this. At least six of Ortega's books have been available in paperback, why not *The Revolt of the Masses?*

If Ortega's book has actually been ignored, I believe it is because his analysis of our age comes too close to the truth for our comfort and peace of mind. Americans have no relish for criticism which cuts at the roots of their society and culture. Their attitude toward such criticism is largely defensive, and what better defense than quietly ignoring this book? Ortega offends us deeply when he says that America is "the paradise of the masses." He sees us as a bunch of witless, conceited, mediocrities, and he predicts that the result of all our "progress" is going to be a new and terrible form of barbarism. On top of insulting us, Ortega scares us when he says that as "mass-men" we will use the terrible weapons now at our disposal against anyone who tries to restrain us. According to Ortega the "mass-man" is the "spoiled child" of history, and isn't it true that the United States is acting like a spoiled child (Russia is another) when she uses the threat of atomic attack to get her own way?

Edward Gibbon, the historian of the decline and fall of Rome, was convinced that the fall of Rome could never have taken place under modern conditions. He argued that the barbarians who destroyed Rome would have to become civilized before they could use modern weapons. Never again, he said, could barbarism make inroads on the civilized world. He never suspected that the new barbarism would arise in the midst of civilization itself. On all sides Ortega sees well-meaning people struggling to ameliorate the effects of this vertical invasion of barbarism — juvenile delinquency, dope addiction, drunkenness, vice, crime, violence, brutality, moral nihilism — meanwhile the tide of savagery rises in the streets of every city. I know some people will refuse to believe this, but they would not be so foolish as to venture into New York's Central Park jungle at night.

Americans by and large simply have no stomach for reading the things that Ortega dishes up for them in *The Revolt of the Masses*. "Negative" and "pessimistic" they call them, and, like the true mass-men they are, they feel free to reject anything they do not like. Nor is Ortega's book the only one of its kind being given the silent treatment for having raised spectres which trouble our self-complacency and shallow optimism. There has never been a paperback edition of Erich Fromm's *The Escape from Freedom*, nor of Waldo Frank's *Rediscovery of America* (which has not been off the library shelf for twenty-five years at the college where I teach.) Both of these books contain the kind of trenchant criticism for which we ignore Ortega's book. We apparently believe that the truth should always be something pleasant and we will no doubt go on thinking so until the end.

The most important thing in *The Revolt of the Masses* is Ortega's description of the emergence and rise to social domination of what he calls "the mass-man," the new barbarian created by industrialism and its attendant leap of population. Europe grew from 180 million to 460 million in a single century; the United States grew from 25 million to 90 million in the same period. Ortega explains that when men appear on the scene so fast, and in such large numbers, it is impossible to educate them. They can be taught to use machines and other modern instruments, but not to understand them. They have no sense of history or of the highly complex problems of civilization. So far as they know the world began with them, and they are ready to rule it. In other words, the mass-man, the modern barbarian, takes civilization for granted as something given. Like the savage in the jungle, he assumes that it has always been there, and will always be there, no matter what he does.

Furthermore, says Ortega, this mass-man is perfectly content to be just like everyone else. He regards himself as superior without making any effort to perfect himself because he thinks he is already complete and he is perfectly satisfied with himself as he is. The real social revolution is that "the commonplace mind, knowing itself to be commonplace, has the assurance to proclaim the rights of the commonplace and to impose them where it will. The mass crushes beneath it everything that is different, everything that is excellent, individual, qualified and select. Anybody who is not like everybody, who does not think like everybody, runs the risk of being eliminated. As they say in the United States, 'to be different is to be indecent.'" Ortega thus describes the triumph of mediocrity.

He finds that the mass mentality has permeated all levels of society, which means that the things he has described are not confined to the lower levels of society. I cannot answer for all levels of society, but I see plenty of evidence around me that many teachers have mass minds. When a man with a mass mentality reads, says Ortega, "he does so with a view, not of learning something from the writer, but rather of pronouncing judgment on him when he is not in agreement with the commonplaces that the reader carries in his head." Ortega is quite blunt on this point: "If you read like this," he says to his reader, "you have a mass mind." I blushed when I first read that: I had to face it, like many teachers (and a great many of their students who imitate them) I was clearly in this category.

It is ironical that education, which ought to insure us against the self-sufficiency, conceit, and vulgarity of the mass mentality, no longer can be counted on to do so. In fact it is far more likely to work against anyone who desires to achieve individuality and excellence. The reason, Ortega explains, is that education, as every aspect of our intellectual life, has come under the domination of science, a domination which becomes increasingly strong as time passes. Science has received, and doubtless will continue to receive, an ever-increasing proportion of time, effort, money, and prestige. Its influence is so pervasive, its prestige so great, that even teachers of such unlikely subjects as literature and philosophy have yielded to the temptation of gaining respect by becoming "scientific." The influence of science in education, therefore, is twofold: what it does to the scientists themselves, and what it does to those who ape the "scientific" approach, no matter how inappropriate it is to the subjects they study and teach.

As for the scientists, Ortega believes that "the actual scientific man is the prototype of the mass-man." Ortega explains that science creates mass-men, "not by chance, not through the individual failings of each particular man of science, but because science itself — the root of our civilization — automatically converts him into mass-man, makes of him a primitive, a modern barbarian." He goes on to say that in large part this is due to the effects of specialization. (I shall have something to say about the similar effects of specialization on teachers of literature later on.)

Ortega explains that many scientific tasks can be done by almost anybody. The method employed is to divide the work up into small parts, and to concentrate on one small part, leaving the rest to others. The work proceeds mechanically, and it is not even necessary for the operator to understand fully the principles which govern his work. When a new fact of nature discovered in this way is added to other facts, it really does constitute knowledge, says Ortega. But the specialist who discovered the new fact cannot lay claim to this knowledge. He knows only his small part; he is radically ignorant of all the rest.

"Here," says Ortega, "we have a precise example of this strange new man whom I have attempted to define. I have said he was a human product unparalleled in history. The specialist serves as a

28

striking example, making clear to us the radical nature of the novelty. For, previously, men could be divided simply into the learned and the ignorant, those more or less the one, and those more or less the other. But your specialist cannot be brought in under either of these two categories. He is not learned, for he is formally ignorant of all that does not enter into his speciality; but neither is he ignorant, because he is a 'scientist,' and 'knows' very well his own tiny portion of the universe. We shall have to say that he is a learned ignoramus, which is a very serious matter, as it implies that he is a person who is ignorant, not in the fashion of the ignorant man, but with all the petulance of one who is learned in his own special line."

I find that a perfectly marvellous description of the specialist, and it doesn't apply just to scientific specialists. "By specializing the scientist," Ortega goes on to say, "civilization has made him hermetic and self-satisfied within his limitations; but this very inner feeling of dominance and worth will induce him to wish to predominate outside his speciality, and the result is that he will behave in almost all spheres of life as does the mass-man." G. B. Shaw put all this much more succinctly when he said that "no man can be a pure specialist without being in the strict sense an idiot." How many students will become specialists without ever realizing this for the simple reason that all of their teachers are pure specialists?

Now for the influence of science and specialization on other realms of intellectual life. In his *Irrational Man*, William Barrett describes how Anglo-American philosophy has, under the domination of science, become almost exclusively devoted to the "scientific" philosophy of Logical Positivism. In the eyes of the Logical Positivist, Barrett asserts, "man is a curious creature who dwells in the tiny island of light composed of what he finds scientifically 'meaningful,' while the whole surrounding area in which ordinary men live from day to day and have their dealings with other men is consigned to the outer darkness of the 'meaningless.'"

The self-limiting nature of science is very precisely stated by Wittgenstein, who maintains that in science "when an answer cannot be expressed, neither can the question be expressed." A scientist would say that since science cannot possibly answer any question about the human spirit, for example, therefore all questions regarding it are inadmissible. This principle may be all right for science, but for philosophy! When the same principle is applied to beauty, love, to all manifestations of the human spirit, the result is a philosophy for robots, not men.

Barrett goes on to attack Logical Positivism for being as limited in its way as Marxian dialectical materialism. He claims that both give us a thin and oversimplified picture of man since they have "not yet come to terms with the shadow side of human life." I believe that Barrett is right. In a similar way scientific objectivity and specialization have narrowed the outlook of teachers of literature, many of whom pride themselves on their "scientific" methods, and exhibit many of the characteristics which Barrett accuses the Logical Positivists of, as well as many of the attributes of the mass mentality of scientific specialists.

Since we take a scientific view of everything, including literature, in everything we tend to deny the spiritual side of man. As a result, we have become terribly confused about what is real. In *The Screwtape Letters*, C. S. Lewis points out that men today believe that in "all experiences which can make them happier or better only the physical facts are 'real,' while the spiritual elements are 'subjective'; in all experiences which can discourage or corrupt them the spiritual elements are the main reality, and to ignore them is to be an escapist. Thus in birth the blood and pain are 'real,' the rejoicing a mere subjective point of view; in death, the terror and ugliness reveal what death 'really means.' The hatefulness of a hated person is 'real' — in hatred you see men as they are, you are disillusioned; but the loveliness of a loved person is merely a subjective haze concealing a 'real' core of sexual appetite or economic association."

Bingo! Mr. Lewis has us down pat. Just look around you and you will see plenty of examples of these wild contradictions. Any man today can advocate in public, and in plain language, the deprivation of rights to Negroes and other racial groups, flogging,

30

castration of the unfit, capital punishments of the most degrading kind, even the use of genocidal weapons; but just let a novelist, poet, or even a teacher of literature open his mouth in defense of a moral or spiritual ideal, and we accuse him of disturbing the peace.

As far as the study of literature is concerned, perhaps H. W. Garrod hit the truth when he said that we are really afraid of what literature might do to us. We want to admire it, enjoy it, exploit it, but when it asks *us* to do something — to become better than we are, we reject it with scorn and abuse. We reject, too, any suggestion that literature ought to make us better. No definition of the purpose of literature is hooted at so much as Matthew Arnold's, that literature is "a criticism of life," which, by enabling us to see life "as in itself it really is, teaches us how to live." According to Arnold, and this part of his theory is usually ignored, literature also enables a man "to find his own soul, his true and permanent self, which is man's chief concern in life, for this is the secret of happiness."

One reason why Arnold's idea of learning to live from literature is held up to ridicule is that the study of literature has become almost exclusively the concern of professional specialists who make a living producing more professional specialists like themselves. This is the reason the tail of graduate studies so often wags the departmental dog. Today the word "amateur," which used to apply to someone who does a thing for the love of it, someone who "takes pleasure in what is for others a commendable ordeal," as Jacob Burckhardt puts it, has become a term of abuse.

But professionalism is inescapably a form of specialization, and specialization is inescapably a process whereby a man limits himself by directing all his capabilities in one direction. To be human, however, as even the professional specialists admit in their official propaganda, is to develop one's capabilities in all directions, to become "a whole man," "many-sided," "well-rounded," or perhaps nearer the truth of the matter, though this does not appear in official pronouncements, "childlike, curious, complex, and immoral," as Oskar, the runt hero of Gunter Grass's *The Tin Drum* says.

Granted that some form of specialization is needed if we are to get things done in science and scholarship, I fail to see why the professional specialists who teach literature feel obliged to force even undergraduates into the professional mold. Because of this the present system of teaching literature at the college level produces carbon copies of the professional specialists who teach it, but it fails miserably in convincing the non-professional student that the study of literature is important, and nobody seems to mind very much.

It seems to me that if the professional specialists could just forget their training (which made them into carbon copies), possibly they could be made to realize that by confining their teaching to the narrow limits of their professional interests they are doing their best to destroy its one vital purpose. It is true that they are doing no more than specialists in other subjects, but they are doing far more damage to their subject because literature is the one subject being taught in college which is, or ought to be, exclusively concerned with each student as a person. All other subjects are devoted to understanding something else: science to nature, history to the past, psychology to human behavior, and so on. Literature alone offers the student a chance to discover who he is, what kind of a person he is, and what kind of life he ought to live. Literature ought to do this for *all* students, not just English majors — the pity is that it doesn't do it even for them, and perhaps for them least of all.

I would like to be able to report that American teachers of literature are aware of the limitations of the professional approach to literature, and are about to do something about it. I would like to be able to report this, but I can't. Teachers today are not only orthodox in politics and economics (thanks largely to loyalty oaths which take away their right to speculate about these matters), but they are socially, intellectually, and professionally orthodox as well. They are not critical of the system which produced them, nor of their own activities within that system. Apart from a few malcontents who feel that their most cherished professional aims (pay raises, promotion, and publication) have been slighted, an air of complacency reigns in English departments across the country. There is just enough carping and squabbling going on to disguise the fact that nobody, and I mean nobody, wants to throw down the entire system of impersonal, objective, intellectualism — which is just what is needed.

Like my colleagues, before I finished going to school I had absorbed a certain amount of expert opinion about literature. In America every person who has a Ph. D. degree is considered an "expert" in something or other, though a week before he gets it he is not listened to with much respect. I had also developed a certain skill in speaking and writing about literature, the subject I was becoming an "expert" in myself. But the one thing which would have made all the difference was lacking: literature had not become a part of my life. It is true enough that I was able to read a novel; analyze, evaluate, and judge it; speak and write about it; dish it up *a la mode,* so to speak; but seldom or ever was this more to me than a lifeless intellectual exercise, a display of my cleverness.

The notion that literature ought to be a part of life; that unless one is somehow different after having experienced a work of art the experience is meaningless; none of this had occurred to me, nor, so far as I was aware, to any of my teachers or associates. Had the idea been raised among us, I suspect that we would have been scornful (though perhaps without clearly understanding why). I have long since taken my place in academic ranks as a teacher of literature, and still I feel some reluctance to put forth the idea that true culture ought to make us different, even better, than we are. My colleagues are cultured according to their own standards (according to mine many of them are merely professional specialists), and if I suggested that their culture may have missed the point, I would be advised to "Stop talking rot, for God's sake!"

I may as well admit it, this insistence on a personal involvement in culture sounds a little like rot to me too. After all I was brought up in the same way. But I can see perfectly well that the kind of culture in which only the opinions of the "expert" command respect is not going to mean very much to anyone, least of all to the experts themselves. Culture for them is, in Toynbee's phrase, "an instrument of worldly ambition or of frivolous amusement." Furthermore, specialization and professionalism lead to a kind of Brahmin intel-

33

lectualism: a good many teachers of literature, for example, regard themselves as guardians of the cultural temple. Like any priesthood they cannot believe that a mere layman can be initiated in cultural rites without their help.

Oswald Spengler, in a playful mood, compares the academic world to the Catholic Church. "In all the specialist sciences, medicine and lecture-room philosophy included, there are fully developed hierarchies leading up to school popes, grades, and dignities (the doctor's degree as an ordination), sacraments and councils. The uninitiate is rigorously treated as the 'layman,' and the idea of a generalized priesthood residing in the believers themselves is passionately combated. The language of learning was originally Latin, but today all sorts of special languages have formed themselves which (in the domain of radioactivity, for example, or that of the law of contract) are unintelligible save to those who have received the higher initiation."

In the academic world, Spengler goes on to say, "There are founders of sects, such as many of Kant's and Hegel's disciples were; there are missionaries to the unbelievers, like the Monists. There are heretics, like Schopenhauer and Nietzsche, there is the weapon of the ban, and there is the Index in the form of the Conspiracy of Silence. There are ethical truths and dogmas, a ritual in the citation of orthodox writings, and even a scientific sort of beatification. After death the teachers of error are excluded from the eternal bliss of the text-book and cast into the purgatorial fires of foot-notes, whence, purged by the intercession of the believer, they ascend into the paradise of the paragraph."

All very amusing, but with bite. As for myself, I am less in love with my role in this cultural priesthood than I used to be. Perhaps this is because I have begun to realize that we have lost two precious things in our culture of the specialist and the expert — perspective and innocence. For one thing I do not believe that it is possible to be simple and straightforward any more — no one will listen. For another I believe that we have succeeded in dehumanizing our culture, as Ortega y Gasset predicted. If this is true, isn't it the loss of a kind of innocence? We seem to have forgotten what even

Dostoevsky's Raw Youth knew: "What is simplest is never understood till the last, when everything that is cleverer or stupider has been tried already."

One meets many very clever, sophisticated, and highly-educated people today, but how many of them have any sense of proportion; how many try, in Arnold's words, "to see life steadily and to see it whole"? Among no other people has specialization been pushed farther than with us; no other people have become so fragmented, so neurotic, so basically lacking in balance. As a result, our intellectuals have a ready answer for everything, and a solution for practically nothing — least of all their own personal problems. Though unlamented, the losses due to our sophistication of culture have been considerable. If nothing else, it has made us forget another of Dostoevsky's simple truths: "People, as a general rule, are much more naive and simple hearted than we suppose, and we ourselves are too."

CHAPTER IV

MAN vs MACHINE

Lewis Mumford has objected to the kind of education which prepares men and women to perform the multitude of specialized tasks which are necessary to keep a complex technological and industrial society in motion. In effect, said Mumford, they are turned into cogs, levers, and rods in a vast machine. It is true that without them the machine could no longer function, but everyone becomes less human in the process. As Norbert Wiener points out, "When human atoms are knit into an organization in which they are used, not in their full right as responsible human beings, but as cogs and levers and rods, it matters little that their raw material is flesh and blood. *What is used as an element in a machine, is in fact an element in the machine.*" Like Mumford, Wiener questions the value and purpose of a society which can exist only at the expense of dehumanization, a society in which men "are tolerated only to the extent that they take on the attributes of machines."

Mumford interprets Dostoevsky's *Notes from Underground* as a warning that if science and technology succeed in making man over in the image of the machine, the human spirit, unable to assert itself in any other way, will do so in crime, in deliberate outbreaks of torture and sadism. There is plenty of evidence of this already. I am amazed that Dostoevsky could foresee so clearly that the cult of the machine and the depersonalization of man would bring out the demonic and primitive in us, turning loose elements of violence and irrationality that could easily disrupt the entire structure of our civilization. And Dostoevsky is not the only writer who has seen this. As Mumford says, "Thinkers of the most diverse backgrounds have realized that the unqualified cult of mechanism leads to nihilism; and nihilism, even if it were not equipped with the atom bomb and the H-bomb, would be capable of bringing to an end, not merely our civilization, but the human race itself."

It is true that while most of us today are bursting with pride over the material progress of the 20th century, and the promise of more of the same in the future, there is a kind of "progress" of which we are not so proud, the progress in horror, bloodshed, torture, and beastliness, the threat of a renewed barbarism which is emerging from within our civilization. Sigmund Freud portrayed human existence as a struggle between Death, the dark instincts of aggression and self-destruction in man; and Eros, the spirit of light, love, and life. "Men have brought their powers of subduing the forces of nature to such a pitch that by using them they could now very easily exterminate one another to the last man," he wrote in *Civilization and its Discontents.* "Men know this, hence arises a great part of their current unrest, their dejection, their mood of apprehension."

Even before the bomb Freud saw that our age would come more and more under the threat of the tremendous, deadly, unseen forces which lurk in the night side of the human soul. Our greatest danger is that lulled by comforts and pleasures beyond the wildest dreams of men throughout history, we will listlessly permit these forces to prevail. If this comes to pass, nothing will remain of man, least of all the brilliant scientific and technological achievements which have, in the end, reduced him to the hapless victim of his own powers of absolute destruction.

Are men like Freud and Dostoevsky right? My reading of history convinces me that they are. One of the astounding and totally unexpected results of our age of reason and science has been the emergence of a new and terrible barbarism. In the streets of our large cities more savages appear every day. These modern savages have only one answer to their frustrations, their anxieties, their rages — violence! The assassination of President Kennedy has provided us

37

with one recent example, the murder of his assassin another, and the pitiless television scrutiny of these events still a third.

Of these three acts of violence, that committed by television was by far the worst because it involved us all. Like the true mass-men we are, we never question our absolute right to see everything that is going on. We seem to have no real sense of decency left. On the surface we were shocked and grieved at what we saw, but there was plenty of morbid curiosity underneath. The horror of Kennedy, Oswald, and Ruby did not satisfy us. We had to have a peek at the murdered policeman's widow, see her real anguish, her real terror and panic, see her reduced to abjection under the brutal questioning of a reporter. "You did love your husband very much, didn't you?" "You will miss him, won't you?" "How are you going to manage now that he is dead?" "What will become of you and the children?"

It is true that a lot of tender-hearted viewers sent money, and no doubt this is the reason the widow allowed herself to be used to satisfy our morbidity. But what about the rest of us? We are no better than those Romans for whom life became one continuous circus. The only difference is that we are armed with a peeping-tom machine which reduces the entire world to the arena of our show, an arena in which nothing, least of all human dignity, is sacred.

The unpleasant fact is that the tide of violence in our lives is rising, and will continue to rise. I do not believe that anyone — perhaps psychologists and sociologists least of all — anticipated the strangest contradiction of all, that crimes of violence and suicide continue to increase with prosperity. One reason is that we are living in a machine-dominated, rather than a man-dominated world. The machine, a product of reason, demands reasonable behavior from all who serve it — anyone who drives a car soon learns this, or ends up on a slab. One consequence is that the non-rational side of man has no outlet in a machine-dominated culture. Therefore it manifests itself in any way it can, insanity, alcoholism, perversion, suicide, murder. This is why we have so much violence today, and why this violence is on the increase.

The idea is far from new. One hundred and fifty years ago

Goethe warned that man would be enslaved and destroyed by the machine. Goethe's Faust bartered his soul with Mephistopheles, as we have bartered ours with science and technology, for sensual gratification, wealth, and power. Goethe saw technical and material progress as a way of living "in which the next moment devours the preceding one," in which no traditions are established, or can be established, in which men live according to the rhythm of machines because human rhythms cannot be established without traditions. Goethe foresaw that the emancipation of the intellect (the machine is a product of pure intellect) would create just the sort of world we live in today: a world of great abundance, great comfort, great danger, and great fear. In *Wilhelm Meister* he portrayed "the repairman," a mindless and soulless automaton who had every characteristic of the modern mass-man.

In our own time Elmer Rice has given us a picture of what the machine has done to man in his comedy, *The Adding Machine.* One of the interesting things about Rice's play is that it involves automation. This means that the play gets more significant as time passes. Automation is the next crisis that capitalism must face. Marx predicted that capitalism would fall of its own weight because it has never succeeded in solving the problem of distributing the goods it produces in such abundance. Overproduction is ruinous. Time and automation will reveal if Marx is right. Meanwhile let us look at Rice's comedy.

The "hero" of *The Adding Machine* is Mr. Zero, a middle-aged bookkeeper who loses his job when his boss replaces him with an adding machine. When the boss tells Zero that he is no longer needed (just when Zero was expecting a raise in recognition of his twenty-five years of service), Zero is so overcome by frustration and rage that he picks up a spike bill-file and pushes it into his boss's heart. Rice treats Zero's murderous rage very sympathetically. If I understand him correctly, Rice regards this as the last vestige of humanity in Zero. This is the reason he sends Zero to the Elysian Fields after his execution.

The "heaven" that Zero finds himself in is a very strange place. To get there all you have to do is prove you are human — which isn't so easy in our world. Zero had to kill in order to prove it. In the Elysian Fields Zero soon finds out what kind of people he will have to associate with, and he doesn't like it. "They seem to think of nothing but enjoyment or of wasting their time in profitless occupations." Zero's training in an industrialized society has taught him to regard pleasure and idleness as the deadliest of sins. As he puts it, "Some paint pictures from morning to night, or carve blocks of stone. Others write songs or put words together, day in and day out. Still others do nothing but lie under the trees and look at the sky. There are men who spend all their time reading books and women who think only of adorning themselves. And forever they are telling stories and laughing and singing and dancing. There are drunkards, thieves, vagabonds, blasphemers, adulterers." To Zero these people are "a lot of rummies an' loafers an' bums," and he wants no part of them. He leaves immediately for the other place.

The "other place" is as strange as Rice's heaven. Here Zero is put to work for another twenty-five years on an adding machine. At the end of this time he is told that he is to be sent back to earth for the last time (he has been back and forth fifty thousand times at least — each time getting a little worse, a little less human.) After this last incarnation, his soul is to be scrapped — he is not worth saving. His new life on earth is described to him: "There'll be millions like you. You'll be a baby again, and then when you get a little older you'll begin to learn things — and you'll learn all the wrong things and learn them all in the wrong way. By that time you'll be ready for school. There they'll tell you the truth about a great many things that you don't give a damn about and they'll tell you lies about all the things you ought to know — and about all the things you want to know they'll tell you nothing at all. When you get through you'll be equipped for your life's work. You'll be ready to take a job."

When Zero is told what his job is to be, he is to operate a vast bookkeeping machine with his big toe, he says that his new life doesn't sound so bad. Then he is told the truth about himself: "You're a failure, Zero, a failure. A waste product. A slave to a contraption of steel and iron. The animal's instincts, but not his strength and skill. The animal's appetites, but not his unashamed indulgence of them. The ready prey of the first jingo or demagogue or political adventurer who takes the trouble to play upon your ignorance and credulity and provincialism. You poor, spineless, brainless boob."

If we take Zero to be representative of the common man in an industrialized society, which is clearly Rice's intention, then what is the message of *The Adding Machine?* The message, I would say, is that man has lost his way: he has become the "slave to a contraption of steel and iron"; he is lower than the animals, and he is destined for extinction. Rice indicates how Zero can save himself, but to Zero the means of salvation seem worse than damnation, this is why he leaves the Elysian Fields. The remedy Rice proposes is to throw off all the moral restraints on which our society rests — nothing short of this. If we are to have a heaven on earth, and if this heaven is to be patterned after Rice's, then idleness, debauchery, even murder will be accepted as human; what will lead men to perdition are the things we regard as virtues: sobriety, thrift, chastity, respectability, dilligence. What Rice seems to be saying is that we must exalt vice and cast out virtue; at least that is what he says to me, and I must say that like Zero I do not relish it. I am no prude, but a society without a moral basis strikes me as an abomination. Therefore I am left with this question: What on earth is Rice getting at in this play?

I puzzled over this question for a long time before I came up with an answer. I believe that Rice is telling us that the only way we can escape the inexorable processes of dehumanization we are undergoing is by attacking the moral standards which permitted them to grow in the first place, and which allow them to continue. Rice's attitude is apparent in the description he gives of Zero's next life on earth: "You'll eat the wrong food and wear the wrong clothes and you'll live in swarming dens where there's no light and no air! You'll learn to be a liar and bully and a braggart and a coward and a sneak. You'll learn to fear sunlight and to hate beauty." To me, Rice seems to be saying that if man had not been persuaded that it was wrong to enjoy life, to make all the pleasures

41

of the senses into vices, then he would never have permitted the world to become the hideous nightmare that it is.

History, I believe, bears him out: the Puritan revolution preceded the Industrial Revolution, and without the Puritan virtues of hard work, thrift, and distrust of pleasure; and without the tremendous energy generated by turning man's mind against his body; the Industrial Revolution would not have been possible. Man would not have been content to make the necessary sacrifices, he would not have had the single-minded devotion to his work had his life not been deprived of joy; above all, he would not have stood for the drabness of life in an industrialized world had he not been taught, like Zero, to fear sunlight and to hate beauty. The difference between what life today might have been, and what it is, is the difference between Chaucer's England of perpetual Maytime, and T. S. Eliot's wasteland, where April, which "breeds lilacs out of the dead land," is "the cruelest month," reminding us of the drabness and sterility of our lives.

Our present system of morality is based on the assumption, a hold-over from the days of our Puritan forefathers, that every natural function of the body is degrading. A curious assumption considering that our very existence is far more dependent upon these despised functions than upon the exalted functions of the mind. Our morality, however, so far from recognizing this simple fact, places the mind in ascendency over the body, and imposes upon it the stern police duty of making the body "behave" according to a set of rules which demand that the bodily appetites be denied, misdirected, or, when permitted, strips them of all normal satisfactions.

Nietzsche accused the church of having perverted man's attitude toward sex until "sin" has become a synonym for sex. As a consequence whole generations of Christians have been reproducing themselves with a guilty conscience. The conviction that we are sinning in our sex stirs up our nervous energies, true, but the waste of spiritual energy is appalling. Instead of harmonious concord of our mental and physical functions, we are torn by a deadly struggle of mind and body for supremacy. There is no doubt in my mind that this is at the root of our present-day neuroticism.

As Rice points out, a great part of the disharmony in our lives can be attributed to the way we are being educated. When Zero has been taught to fear sunlight and to hate beauty, Rice says, then he is ready for school. It will not matter then how much education he gets, nothing he will ever be taught will correct his distorted and inhuman view of the world. The very subjects which profess to "well-round" him, the humanities, are not only uninterested in his emotions and his bodily functions, they regard them as academically out of bounds.

The humanities may profess to be interested in the whole man, but in reality they are only interested in him from the ears up. The rest is considered not quite nice. In disproof of their claims, humanities teachers produce as many neurotics as any others. You cannot drive out "fear" and "hatred" by appealing to the intellect alone. It takes an emotion to overcome an emotion — that's Spinoza's saying. Zero would have to be taught to respond to the warmth of sunlight, a physical response, and to love beauty, an emotion. But how can education give him these things when it has banished the body and ignores the emotions?

If we truly respected and accepted the body and all its works, perhaps we would not try to avoid intense emotions whenever we can. Some people I know deny that we do this — some people will deny anything. Melvin Tumin, at least, calls them as he sees them: "Real feeling is viewed with distrust and hostility because it almost always means bad manners, spontaneity, unpredictability, lack of realism, failure to observe routines. Above all, there is the question of form. One can't play it cool if he insists on the validity of his feelings. To play it hot is bad form. Bad form is worse than halitosis. Well-rounded, adjusted, happy — these are the things we are told it is important for us to be. No points, no sharp cutting edges, no despairs and elations."

When we feel that we are too sad, too lonely, too depressed, and our tolerance for these so-called "negative emotions" is very small, we take a little pill. If we have anything important to do, decisions to make, appointments to keep, a party to go to, we take

43

two little pills — one to calm us down, one to pep us up. We want to be at our "best": cool, calm, calculating, impersonal, unfeeling — in short, as unemotional as machines. If we have any big problems, we would prefer to turn them over to an electronic brain which doesn't feel anything at all. The inhuman has become our ideal.

No one is going to deny that this kind of behavior is very much in keeping with the business-like society we live in. Nevertheless it is very bad for man himself. Our world wags on very well, producing more and more, faster and faster, but we find ourselves less and less at home in it. This is precisely Rice's point, or I miss my guess. We have all become Zeros, more or less, otherwise we could not fail to see the enormity of a culture in which the machine is making man over in its image.

The machine's transformation of man is the theme of C. Virgil Gheorghiu's novel, *The 25th Hour*. No other book I have read portrays the modern fall of man more powerfully than this one. Judged as a novel, it is not very good; but some things take precedence over literary criticism, a simple truth which most critics scrupulously ignore. *The 25th Hour* is a terrifying book, as the reader can judge for himself. Here is a part of it.

"A society which contains millions of millions of mechanical slaves and a mere two thousand million humans — even if it happens to be the humans who govern it — will reveal the characteristics of its proletarian majority. In the Roman Empire the slaves spoke, worshiped, and loved according to the customs they had brought with them from Greece, Thrace, or other occupied countries. The mechanical slaves of our own civilization retain their characteristics and live according to the laws governing their nature. This nature, or, if you prefer it, this technological reality, exists within the framework of contemporary society. Its influence is becoming more and more dominant.

"In order to make use of their mechanical slaves men are obliged to get to know them and to imitate their habits and laws. Every employer has to learn something of the language and habits of his employees to be able to give orders. Conquerors, when they are numerically inferior to the conquered, will almost always adopt

44

the language and customs of the occupied nations, for the sake of convenience or for other practical reasons — and that in spite of the fact that they are the masters. The same process is working itself out in our own society, even though we are unwilling to recognize it. We are learning the laws and the jargon of our slaves, so that we can give them orders. And so, gradually and imperceptibly, we are renouncing our human qualities and our own laws. We are dehumanizing ourselves by adopting the way of life of our slaves.

"The first symptom of this dehumanization is contempt for the human being. Modern man assesses by technical standards his own value and that of his fellow men; they are replaceable component parts. Contemporary society, which numbers one man to every two or three dozen mechanical slaves, must be organized in such a way as to function according to technological laws. Society is now created for technological, rather than for human requirements. And that's where tragedy begins. Men are suddenly being forced to live and behave according to technological laws that are foreign to them. Those who do not respect the laws of the machine — now promoted to social laws — are punished.

"Man, living in a minority, gradually develops into a proletarian minority. He is excluded from the society to which he belongs but in which he can no longer be integrated. As a result, he grows an inferiority complex, a desire to imitate the machine and to rid himself of those specifically human characteristics which hold him at a distance from the center of social activity. This slow process of dehumanization is at work under many different guises, making man renounce his emotions and reducing social relationships to something categorical, automatic, and precise, like the relationship between different parts of a machine. The rhythm and the jargon of the mechanical slaves, or robots, if you like, find echoes in our social relationships and our administration, in painting, literature, and dancing. Men are becoming the apes of robots."

At this point Gheorghiu quotes Keyserling to the effect that "life has no objective aim, unless it be death. Every real and true aim is always subjective." Dostoevsky's Underground Man said that "two times two makes four is the beginning of death." I never understood what he meant before.

Gheorghiu continues: "The technocrats of Western civilization attempt to impose an objective aim on life. That is the best way of annihilating it. They have reduced life to a series of statistics. But statistics inevitably leave out of account the case that is unique of its kind. The more humanity develops, the more decisive will be the particular uniqueness of each individual person and each individual case. Contemporary society is moving in precisely the opposite direction. Everything is reduced to generalities.

"It is in attempting to generalize and to seek or find all values in generalities that Western man has lost all sense of the value of the unique, of that which takes individual life as a starting point. Hence the great danger of collectivism, whether interpreted in the Russian or the American way.

"Herein lies the crime of Western Technological Civilization. It kills the living man, sacrificing him to plans, theories, and abstractions. Here we have the modern variant of human sacrifice. The stake and the *auto-da-fe* have passed away, but in their place stand bureaucracy and statistics, the two present-day social myths whose flames consume the sacrifice of human flesh.

"Human life has no meaning unless it is conceived as a whole. We can only grasp its ultimate purpose if we bring into play the same senses that help us to understand religion and to interpret or to create art. In the search of the ultimate end of life reason plays only a secondary role. Mathematics, statistics, and logic are as ineffectual, as guides to the comprehension and organization of human life, as they are to the appreciation of Raphael or Beethoven. But our modern Western society persists in trying to arrive at an understanding of Beethoven and Raphael by means of mathematics and calculations. It is relentless in its efforts to improve men's lives by resorting constantly to statistics.

"These attempts are both ridiculous and tragic. The most that man could achieve under this system would be an acme of social perfection. But it would not help him in the least. Once his life has been reduced to its social and automatic element and subjected

46

entirely to the laws of the machine, it will simply have ceased to exist. These laws can never under any circumstances give life its meaning, and if life is deprived of its meaning — its only meaning and one that is totally free, and above and beyond the bounds of logic — then life itself will finally become extinct."

I find it sort of interesting that Gheorghiu, a Romanian, is saying what a Russian, Dostoevsky; a Spaniard, Ortega y Gasset; and an American, Elmer Rice, have said. And all these men of differing nationalities view modern political man as Gheorghiu has described him. Gheorghiu speaks for them all:

"Recently a new species of animal has appeared on the surface of the earth. These animals are called citizens. They do not live in the jungle or the forest, but in offices. Yet they are more ferocious than the beasts of the jungle. They are a bastard breed of man and machine — a degenerate breed, but today the most powerful on earth. Their faces are the faces of men, and outwardly they are indistinguishable from human beings. But soon enough it becomes obvious that they don't behave like human beings. They behave exactly like machines. They have chronometers in place of hearts. Their brain too, is a kind of machine. They are neither machines nor men. Their appetites are those of wild beasts, but they are not wild beasts. They are citizens — a strange mongrel type.

"They have gone forth and multiplied to the ends of the earth. In Russia, since the Communist Revolution, they have created the most advanced branch of Western Technological Civilization. This civilization has taken up all the theories of the West and put them into practice. It has reduced man to zero, in accordance with the doctrine of the West. It has transformed society into one vast machine, in accordance with the doctrine of the West. Russia has imitated the West as only a barbarian or a savage could have done. The only genuinely Russian contribution to Communist society is its barbaric fanaticism: nothing else.

"Apart from bloodthirstiness and fanaticism, every single thing in the USSR comes from the West. That is why a Third World War must be simply a civil war that has broken out and is following its

47

course within the limits of the Technological Civilization of the West. The American and the European aspects of Western civilization will fight the Western Communist aspect."

With our present weapons, this will be a fight to the finish — civil wars are always the bitterest and the bloodiest. What can be done? Very little, says Gheorghiu; in fact, nothing. This shocks us because we operate on the belief that everything can be explained, everything defined, every failure rectified, every problem eventually solved. But there are questions to which there are no answers, problems with no solutions, failures which are final. The Hydrogen bomb is one such problem — we dare not use it, and we dare not give it up.

Long ago Goethe saw that this dilemma would face Western technology: man would find it impossible to live with the machine, and equally impossible to live without it. Perhaps you recall the end of *Faust*. Mephistopheles has been helping Faust reclaim a kingdom from the sea by building a system of dykes. An old couple who have lived on the original shoreline all their lives occupy a cottage which stands on some high ground which Faust wants for a public-works project. Faust tells Mephisto to get rid of them. Mephisto burns down the cottage with the old folks inside. This is just one of his little pranks; he is a tremendous joker.

Faust is infuriated and he sends Mephisto packing; he says he can get along very well without him. But no sooner is Mephisto banished than Faust is visited by four ladies: Dearth, Debt, Care, and Trouble. Faust gets rid of them, but before Care leaves she breaths on Faust and blinds him. As the four ladies go out, their brother, Death, approaches. Faust is dying. Mephisto comes sneaking back with some of his imps to dig a grave for Faust. Faust, now blind hears the digging; he thinks they are working on one of his dykes. "Faster, faster," he orders them. Very ironical.

Faust accomplished what he did only with the help of Mephistopheles; when he dismissed Mephistopheles Faust began to die. Whatever Goethe may have intended by all this, I see very clearly that in actual fact even if, like Faust, we wanted to dismiss our Mephistophelean forces of science and technology, we can't do it.

Our industrial society, with its masses of population, cannot live without these forces, and our population is increasing all the time. It looks, therefore, as if we will have to put up with the pranks.

But not for long if Gheorghiu is right. The significance of his title, *The 25th Hour,* is that Western civilization is already one hour past its final hour. As he puts it: "The twenty-fifth hour is the hour when mankind is beyond salvation — when it is too late even for the coming of the Messiah. It is not the last hour; it is one hour past the last hour. It is Western civilization at this very moment. It is now."

PART II

THE STUDY OF LITERATURE

CHAPTER V

READING FOR BALANCE

In my last chapter, "Man vs Machine," I argued that we are all brought up believing that both the body and the emotions are potential sources of evil, and that it is one of the functions of the intellect to keep them under rigid control. I argued further that this pitting of the mind against the body leads to the imbalance in our lives, an imbalance which causes a great deal of unhappiness and certainly contributes its share to mental illness. In fact a state of imbalance or lack of harmony between the mind and the body is so endemic to this time and this place that I must seek elsewhere for an example of what I mean by a balanced person.

The best example of a man who achieved the kind of balance I have in mind was Goethe. Perhaps the greatest difference between his ideal of life and ours is that he accepted the pleasures of the body and did not think it advisable, as we all do, to suppress his emotions. Goethe had contempt for the puritanical attitude toward the body. He advocated, and practiced, a simple and appreciative acceptance of the body and all the pleasurable sensations to which the gratification of bodily appetites gives rise. What he strove for here, as in all things, was balance: overindulgence of any kind was repugnant to him. If we were to follow Goethe's ideal, our education would prepare us for a lifelong search for balance and harmony among all our faculties, body, mind, and spirit.

Many people I have talked to about this matter regard balance as a kind of stagnation, a condition of no striving. They do not seem to get the point, and I suspect that they do not want to. A man does not simply achieve balance and then stop. He is like a man on a tightrope, just to stay up there takes constant effort. Goethe said at eighty that it had always been a struggle for him to maintain his balance. That he succeeded is demonstrated by the fact that no man ever had a calmer, saner, healthier life. It is not just me who says this, hundreds of other men have said it. And the reader can discover it for himself if he will take the trouble to study Goethe's life and writings.

I cannot say for certain what Goethe, who once expressed his pity for "the poor man to whom the head is everything," would make of our present-day education, but I suspect he would have hated it. In *Wilhelm Meister*, he expresses his conviction that the aim of education is to establish a harmonious relationship between our intellects and our emotions, rather than to develop mere versatility of the intellect. To suppress our emotions, Goethe said, is to overestimate the intellect. To him the emotions had a deep connection with the meaning of life, and they were agents of our growth toward truth. By suppressing the emotions, he maintained, we liberate the intellect; but when we do this the intellect is unrestricted in its objectivity (as in science), and the results will be Mephistophelean anarchy. Anyone who regards this as stupid nonsense has his head in the sand. Where does he think those atomic bombs came from? Any day now the world could be turned into a radioactive wasteland. It is true that man's emotions may pull the triggers, but his intellect created the bombs, there is no denying that.

Perhaps Goethe is right, we have all become Mephistophelean. I have never read a textbook of psychology or sociology which could not have been written by Mephistopheles. And science, which is the greatest creation of man's intellect, has persistently denied any ethical responsibility for its acts. It has so little respect for humanity that it willingly creates weapons of total destruction for a Hitler, a Stalin, or any other madman. Mephistopheles tried to win his bet with Faust by seducing him into precisely this kind of irresponsibility. We too are likely to lose our bet with Mephistophelean science: the strongest emotions we feel amidst all the power and wealth that science has given us are fear and hatred. Love, which counteracts hate, and the courage to be one's self, which alone can banish fear, are taking an unmerciful licking in our world. Heretofore the forces of hate and fear have never been able to prevail over love; armed with the H-bomb, however, they are likely to prove invincible.

If we are to save ourselves from hate and fear, we must somehow revive our capacity to love and to become our true selves. But how many of us are capable of love; how many are aware that the need of *giving* love is even greater than that of *getting* it? On all sides I hear people saying how desperately everyone needs to be loved; but who speaks of the need to love? Camus says that "there is merely bad luck in not being loved; not loving is a calamity." To this I will add that we must all give love, and without expectation of return, for that is the only genuine love. This is the only way we can fill the need of love in ourselves and in others.

Love of others, moreover, is only one kind of love. There is a higher, the highest of which man is capable, love of the good. Love of the good, says Goethe, leads a man beyond himself by making him want what he knows should be, rather than what he desires for himself. The opposite of this is selfishness, or the incapacity to love anyone or anything not even oneself.

I know that most people believe that selfishness is rooted in self-love. Personally I find Erich Fromm's explanation much more enlightening. According to Fromm, the root of selfishness is not self-love, but just the opposite. "The selfish person does not love himself too much, but too little; in fact he hates himself. This lack of fondness and care for himself leaves him empty and frustrated. He is necessarily unhappy and anxiously concerned to snatch from life the satisfactions which he blocks himself from attaining. He seems to care too much for himself but actually he only makes an unsuccessful attempt to cover up and compensate for his failure to care for his real self."

Goethe believed that before anyone can become a person he must learn to love the things of heaven, the things of the earth, and other people. From these three kinds of love comes a fourth, the love of one's self. This love of self, however, is a vastly different thing from the egocentricity we see all around us. Goethe believed that a man could only complete himself when he had fulfilled his personal role in association with, and as a part of, the rest of mankind. "Only mankind in its entirety," he maintained, "is the true man." Each of us can find joy and satisfaction only when we have the courage to feel that we are a part of mankind. His insistence that we do this without surrendering our unique individuality distinguishes his kind of human solidarity from today's conformism and togetherness.

I have said enough now, I believe, to show the great difference between Goethe's ideals of harmonious concord of all our faculties, and of our relationship to our selves and to other men, and our own ideals of mind over body and self-seeking egotism. There is plenty of evidence that our ideals are productive: they drive us relentlessly from achievement to achievement in the service of material progress. We have accomplished things which men not long ago did not even dream were possible. But we seek in vain for some sign of lasting satisfaction with these things, for tranquillity, for contentment. Zeros we find in plenty, but human beings, the one thing that would give the whole rigamarole point and purpose, are rare indeed.

It would be comforting to believe that a good education would enable a man to become one of these rare human beings, but it won't. Our kind of education seems bent on maintaining and even augmenting the imbalance which our industrialized society finds so useful. In the end, the whole responsibility for the task rests upon us alone. We can expect very little help and encouragement. Just the reverse: the one thing we can be absolutely sure of is that men who are mutilated themselves will not be content to see us go through life without a scar. Lewis Mumford contends that being human is regarded today as "a crime more serious than that of sympathizing with Communism." The ultimate security risks, he says, are those "who still retain and still cherish all their human attributes: people who are trusting, tenderhearted, responsive, cooperative, curious, intelligent, humorous, capable of human sympathy and love."

Perhaps it is the most damaging condemnation of the world we live in that those who have managed to remain human are the ones who are certain to be hated, feared, and despised. I have heard young people say that life no longer offers great risks, great adventures, great purpose. There are no more dragons to slay, no more continents to explore, no more Everests to climb. True enough. But a lonely, silent, and deadly struggle is taking place in the soul of man. Let youth dare to be human and it will find plenty of need for its splendid courage, for this is a desperate game played in anguish before empty stands — there is no one there to applaud, no one to praise, no one to record the victories.

How has this situation come about? Lewis Mumford's answer is that "we in America overwhelm the higher functions by constant and never-ending insistence upon the lower ones, just as we will interrupt the music of Bach or Mozart to advertise a cigarette or a laxative. Our life has become an air-conditioned nightmare: packed with sensations and emptied of purposes, glutted with things and starved of meanings; or, rather, we attempt to derive all our meaning and values from the world of dehumanized objects." Mumford believes it is only "by understanding man's whole nature and by fostering constant intercourse between various parts that his balance can be maintained, and his normal growth and development assured. Those who would oppose reason to emotion, as if reason guaranteed integrity and emotion would overthrow it, have learned little about the nature of the human personality."

If what Mumford says is true, then it is obvious that we do not understand the true nature of man, and things will go on as they have until we do. Anton Chekhov said that "if one would make man better, one must make him see what he is." I believe that one way for us to see what we are, perhaps the best way, is to study literature. In literature we see man through the eyes and imagination of the artist. I believe, as James T. Farrell says, that "great and good writers saturate us with a consciousness of life, and, by achieving this effect, endow us with a sense not only of what life

57

is but also what it ought to be." Matthew Arnold said the same thing: literature is a "criticism of life" which teaches us who we are and how we ought to live. If Arnold and Farrell are right, then literature should never be treated as merely a source of pleasant amusement, which is how many people regard it today.

The Greeks, who believed in balance and harmony as a way of life, expected a great deal more from literature than amusement. In *Paideia: The Ideals of Greek Culture,* Werner Jaeger tells us the Greeks believed that "literature has limitless power of converting the human soul — a power which they called *psychagogia.* For art alone possesses the two essentials of educational influence — universal significance and immediate appeal." According to Jaeger, the Greeks were also persuaded that "education and culture are not a formal art or an abstract theory, but a part of life. They held them to be embodied in literature, which is the real expression of all higher culture." Jaeger also says the Greeks believed that "literature cannot be really educative unless it is rooted in the depths of the human soul, unless it embodies a moral belief, a high ardor of the spirit, a broad and compelling ideal of humanity."

The Greeks' "broad and compelling ideal of humanity" was, as I have said, the ideal of balance and harmonious concord of all human faculties. The Greek word for this was *paideia.* Spengler epitomized *our* ideal as *the will to power.* He called Western culture "Faustian," after Goethe's hero who wanted to put the universe in his pocket. Compared to the Greeks, who sought equilibrium, Western man is all thrust, thrust into space, into matter, into mind, and into spirit. The conquest of Everest, flights to the moon, and the Flying Dutchman myth (the spirit of a man condemned to sail endless seas) reveal the nature of our ideal of humanity. Ceaselessly restless (Pascal said that our restlessness is the cause of our unhappiness), we admire and respect only those things, those men, those events which are characterized by excess.

The Greeks, on the other hand, viewed man as a balanced and harmonious whole. The Greek ideal was to leave nothing out, but to avoid all disproportion: both these requirements are essential to their concept of *paideia.* As Camus explains, "The Greeks never carried anything to extremes, neither the sacred nor reason, because they negated nothing, neither the sacred nor reason. They took everything into consideration, balancing shadow with light. We, on the other hand, off in pursuit of totality, are the children of disproportion. We negate beauty, as we negate whatever we do not glorify. And, through all our diverse ways, we glorify but one thing, which is the future rule of reason. In our madness we may go beyond the permissible limits, and at that very moment dark Erinyes will fall upon us and tear us to pieces. Nemesis, the goddess of measure and not revenge, keeps watch. All those who overstep the limits are pitilessly destroyed." Camus also stresses the importance of leaving nothing out, because "if one foregoes a part of what is, one must forego being oneself; one must forego living otherwise than by proxy. There is thus a will to live without rejecting anything of life, which is the virtue I honor most in this world. Few epochs require as much as ours that one should be equal to the best as to the worst in man."

In the greatest Greek poetry, *The Iliad* and *The Odyssey,* and the great tragedies, the bestiality of man is humanized, his monstrosities are divested of their terror, and the ordinary things of life are touched with sublimity. Whatever the Greeks themselves were, they created the healthiest and sanest literature of all time. I believe that anyone who is going to read for balance should certainly include the Greeks. I have an idea that some of this health and sanity rubs off on us. I realize that some people regard this as a crackpot idea, but I can't help that. I expect they wouldn't take balance as a gift; they enjoy being lopsided. Rousseau said that the worst thing about slavery is that even the slaves get used to it. Here we have a similar thing: people get so that they enjoy their imbalance.

I must confess that like many Americans I once had a love affair with the idea of the hundred great books, those books upon which our culture is said to rest. I started reading Mortimer J. Adler's list, which begins with the Greeks. In my ignorance I read bad translations, and I read them badly. I had none of the "background" which teachers of literature regard as essential to our understanding of old books. I was ignorant about Greek language, Greek thought, Greek life, Greek customs, and Greek history — and I still am. Nevertheless I plowed ahead, understanding about a tenth of what I read.

What was the result? I am certainly no "expert" in Greek literature, therefore according to the standards of my profession I wasted my time. But I ended up with just enough balance not to care about that, and with enough sense to look for more. I had also become wise enough to admire Goethe, the last man to practice *paideia*. I learned much more about balance by reading Goethe's books, and even more by studying his life. These are things I couldn't have learned in school from professional experts, because they treat literature as an object, and literature can only teach when it is *felt*, not when it is handled and manipulated as a thing.

One reason Greek literature could teach me balance was that the Greek accounting of man's nature leaves nothing out. The Greeks accepted man's animal nature with an easy tolerance which is impossible for us because of our Puritan traditions. The bawdiness of Aristophanes is a case in point. In his introduction to *Lysistrata*, Eugene O'Neill Jr. explains that making fun of sex "is only what would be expected by anyone candid enough to recognize that the sexual part of human life is the most copious source of the finest humor. It is regrettable and thoroughly human that those persons to whom this fact needs to be pointed out are invariably unwilling or unable to accept it; *Lysistrata* is not for them." I don't know where the idea came from, but a lot of people seem to think that great literature is pure, and what is not pure cannot be great literature. Even a one-eyed reading of *Romeo and Juliet* ought to disabuse them.

There is this to be said: the bawdiness of Aristophanes, like that of Chaucer, is almost pure when compared to the salaciousness of the bedroom scenes which appear in every peeping-tom novel today. The Greek appetite for smut was broad and lusty; ours is finiky and perverted. No one's wit was ever diseased by reading Aristophanes; I cannot say the same for Nabokov's *Lolita*, because mine was. Nor did the Greeks suffer from our obsessive horror of homosexuality. They accepted the plain truth, there have always been and always will be homosexuals. In contrast, our own hysterical efforts to suppress this fact are pitiable.

We have been described as the most sex-ridden people in history. I can believe it. We have inherited the idea that sex is evil, and we measure man by it; no wonder he appears vile. At the same time we have commercialized and exploited sex. In our efforts to suppress sex we have made an obsession of it. This obsession has been seized upon and exploited by advertisers, movie makers, and all sorts of purveyors of mass culture. As a result we are surrounded by advertising, movies, magazines, which are seething with sex. The comics have been spiced up, and even Coke bottles given a sexy shape. We grow up in a world which incites us to the very thing we are taught is sinful. No wonder our nerves are frayed. But sexual instincts have their way of getting even for this double abuse.

Dostoevsky's Prince Valkousky, in *The Insulted and the Injured*, (that's us), says: "If it were possible for every one of us to describe all his secret thoughts, without hesitating to disclose what he is afraid to tell and would not on any account tell other people, what he is afraid to tell his best friends, what, indeed, he is even at times afraid to confess to himself, the world would be filled with such a stench that we should all be suffocated." Each reader must judge the truth of that statement for himself: not many, I expect, can honestly reject it. My point here is that if Dostoevsky is right, perhaps it would be better to accept ourselves for what we are and not grovel in shame and guilt on the one hand, and permit ourselves to be teased and titillated to death by movie makers and advertisers on the other. We cannot possibly find peace of mind as long as we permit our sex to be used against us.

The tragic thing about our attempts to suppress the so-called baser side of our nature is that it inevitably causes us to weaken our highest qualities too. As Nietzsche complained, we are squandering our highest spiritual powers in a vain effort to eradicate our animal nature. The Greeks believed that a man attains his highest spiritual development through accepting the body, not by despising and rejecting it. Goethe's image of man was a being with the head of a

god, and cloven feet — something like the Greek demigod, Pan,
half man, half goat. Wouldn't it be better to simply accept this
duality in man's nature? Have we gotten any closer to heaven
by rejecting it? In turning against our animal part aren't we in
the same fix as the man who, in trying to live without sorrow,
finds his capacity for joy has withered away?

Henry Miller, I believe, has attempted to resurrect this dual
nature of man. In *The Tropic of Cancer,* Miller comments on this:
"Up to the present, my idea in collaborating with myself has been
to get off the gold standard of literature. My idea briefly has been
to present a resurrection of the emotions, to depict the conduct
of a human being in the stratosphere of ideas; that is, in the grip
of delirium. To paint a pre-Socratic being, a creature part goat,
part Titan." Miller's attempt has only been partially successful, I
think. The "Tropic" books are up to his high purpose, and so is
his *Black Spring,* but the three books of *The Rosy Crucifixion,*
"Sexus," "Nexus," and "Plexus," contain many pages which I for
one wish Miller had never written. I can only agree with Lawrence
Durrell who warned Miller that he had gone too far. It is painful
to see a great writer demean himself, no matter how brave his
purpose.

But this is not the reason that most people can't stand Miller's
writing, any of his writing. They don't like it because he dares to
describe all his secret thoughts, and it is true that the world is
filled with a stench that threatens to suffocate us all, just as
Dostoevsky's Valkousky said. Right now, our attitude toward sex
being what it is, we have very little chance of judging Miller's work
fairly. Perhaps he has gone too far the other way; that is, he over-
stresses the animal nature of man.

My guess would be that Dostoevsky comes near to presenting a
balanced view, even though most of his characters strike us as
psychologically grotesque. Our reaction to his characters, however,
may be due to our conception of man as a rational being, a conviction which Dostoevsky emphatically rejects. He believed that the
intellect is only about one-twentieth of man's nature. Because we are
educated in such a way as to make us accept this fraction as the

only thing that counts, we are prepared to understand only about one-twentieth of any character Dostoevsky puts before us.

What Dostoevsky stresses is the astonishing mixture of beauty and ugliness in man, his nobility and his baseness. I like what William Hubben says of Dostoevsky's characters: "We are surprised and appalled at the behavior of his men and women, whose undisguised inward chaos breaks with the pattern of accepted behavior. We see how greatness and viciousness shake man at one and the same time in a moral schizophrenia always known to the New Testament but not yet discovered by the learned philosophers and psychologists of Dostoevsky's time. In his novels, as in the Gospel, the sinner and not the seemingly perfect man surprises us by emerging as the more attractive character, whereas the virtuous man may unexpectedly reveal himself as a base and despairing weakling."

My own feeling about Dostoevsky is that I learned more from him than from any other writer. I thought I knew it all; that I had man, life, and the world all figured out. I was ready for a good shaking up, and Dostoevsky gave it to me. It was a shock, I won't deny it; but my understanding of myself, life, and mankind has deepened. Dostoevsky opened at least one of my eyes.

There is a well-known saying that "in the Kingdom of the Blind the one-eyed man is king." This does not mean that any one-eyed man is better than any blind man; if it does, it is wrong. What it does mean is that a man with one eye can see things a man without eyes cannot see — but the blind man may still be the better man. In the Kingdom of Imbalance in which we live, a conviction that balance is desirable and attainable gives a man his one eye. This will not make him a king; however, he will not spend the rest of his life stumbling around in the dark — that's the important thing.

Starting with the conviction that balance is a good thing, and a desire to strive for it, what can one do to attain it? I wish there were a simple answer; if there is, and I doubt it, I don't know what it is. My way has been to read widely and steadily — in fact I am still at it. Balance is not a given condition; it must be endlessly worked at. What have I read? It gives me a headache even to think about it. A list of the books would be meaningless: many of them I have forgotten, but some of those which made a lasting impression on me have appeared in this book. I read a lot of junk too, but I do not regret it. You cannot be scientific about a thing like this. You have to follow your fancy: any attempt to develop an efficient program of reading for balance is certain to defeat the purpose of it. At least that is my idea.

My conviction is that it doesn't much matter what you read, or where you start reading. If you are seeking in the right direction, you will stumble onto the roads. I know that this sounds haphazard, but that cannot be helped. It would be handy if I could offer a list of books which would guarantee that everyone who read them would increase his chances for inner harmony and contentment, which is what a lot of people seem to be looking for. But I wouldn't give out such a list, even if it were possible, because human "balance" does not mean *contentment*. To be a complete human being you have to hurt sometimes. The books which help you attain this balance are not fairy tales. Besides, the books which work for one person will not work for another — you have to read books intended for *you*. Also the effect of any reading you do will be increased or diminished by your need and by your readiness for it.

Beyond this there is not much advice I can give, except to go on reading, of course. Luck plays a great part in choosing the books which are right for you. Also, as I said — you may have missed the point — you have to be ready for them. I recall that twenty years ago I tried to read Thoreau's *Walden*. Like many young people I gave it up after about two pages, there was nothing in it for me. I read it a short time ago, and it made a deep impression. *Walden* was a fine book for me when I was forty, a disappointing one when I was twenty. Many books, some of the best, are like that; nobody can do anything about it, though teachers sometimes try. Often, too, a book will have an effect on a reader which is disproportionate to its merits. Nobody can do anything about this either, though teachers sometimes try here too. The first books to set my mind on fire were William Saroyan's *The Daring Young Man on the Flying Trapeze,* and his *Inhale and Exhale*. These are not great literature by any means, but I was ready for them and they served.

A great many teachers of literature are very snobbish about what one should read, a big mistake in my estimation. They assume that only the best books can have a good effect on a reader. I find no evidence for this belief. The book that made John Masefield a poet was Du Maurier's *Trilby,* a solid piece of *kitsch.* Henry Miller, who has absolutely no critical sense (this is one of the sources of his vitality and charm as a writer) still goes into raptures over Rider Haggard's *She,* which is even worse trash than *Trilby,* if that's possible. Many of us, I expect, would just as soon forget the books that excited us when we first started to read. Masefield and Miller are merely more grateful and more honest than we are.

Perhaps the best plan for the person who wants to read for balance is to range widely in time and type of books. A great many people spend themselves on trying to keep up with the new books, as if the latest were always the best. I think this is futile. No one today can read everything new there is to read, even in one subject or one kind of literature. Lewis Mumford has even raised the question whether we are not impoverishing ourselves intellectually through overproduction of books and periodicals. He argues that academic advancement depends upon publication ("publish or perish"), hence a great deal of premature and superfluous publication results. To this I would add that the kind of writing and thinking one has to do in order to be published in the learned journals is an incitement to the narrowest kind of pettifogging specialization. These journals are dedicated to the principle of straining at the gnat and swallowing the camel. I occasionally meet teachers of literature who write only for periodicals, and who read little else. Their periodical minds are filled with periodical ideas.

Such readers are trapped in the professional squirrel cage of their specializations. They have to "keep up" in their subject, and this takes all their time — or at least they seem to think it should. They actually feel guilty when they read something which isn't on their subject, because such reading is "unproductive." Such an attitude stems from their conviction, a reasonable one, that if they don't keep up, they will have less chance for professional recognition, promotion, and increases in salary. I know the feeling. But I never intended that this chapter should be devoted to hints on how to be successful at anything else but a human being. If you want to remain human, you cannot give yourself over completely to any specialization without doing yourself a mischief.

Specialization is defended because it is no longer possible for one man to know everything there is to know, not even within the limited range of one discipline, mathematics for example. True enough. But this does not alter the fact that no human being can confine his interests to a single subject for long without permanently damaging his mind and his personality. A lifetime of concentration on a narrow specialization in the humanities, which are supposed to keep us human (or so they are advertised) can turn a man into a wizened academic mole — a strange and wondrous thing to see. The moral is plain: specialization turns even the humanities into processes of dehumanization. More and more graduate programs in the humanities are beckoning students to take up a narrow specialization. If the interests of humanity were to be truly served, every student about to enter graduate school should be warned: "Abandon humanity, all ye who enter here."

Only this remains to be said: no amount of diversity in the books you read will help you to gain balance if you read them with detachment. Reading for balance, so far from being detached, requires ferocious subjectivity of engagement with the author, his ideas, and his work. A very influential teacher of literature, I. A. Richards, believes that "the question of belief or disbelief, in the intellectual sense, never arises when we are reading well. If unfortunately it does arise, either through the poet's fault or our own, we have for the moment ceased to be reading and have engaged in quite a different type of activity." Professor Richards is out of his mind!

It is well for the future of mankind that the influence of teachers rarely extends beyond their lifetime. Richards could not say this unless he regarded literature as "a mere field for the display of virtuosity in the techniques of scholarship — which, taken simply as techniques, are no more worthy of esteem than the technique of building bridges or breeding pigs," as Herbert Hodges said.

George Steiner, in *Tolstoy or Dostoevsky*, raises the crucial question, "Can we dissociate knowledge from belief? Knowledge is the prelude to belief and draws the latter after it. A genuinely neutral mind, moreover, would be closed to that order of literature in which direct appeal is made to our convictions. Neither the *Phaedo* nor *The Divine Comedy* [nor the New Testament, I might add] is intended to leave us impartial. They woo our souls with their argument. Much of great art exacts belief. What we must aim for is to render our imaginations as liberal as possible so that we may respond with scrupulous knowledge and clarity of insight to the possible range of persuasions."

Most teachers of literature I have known are with Richards. I am with Steiner.

CHAPTER VI

READING FOR SELF-DISCOVERY

I have discovered in trying to persuade others of the importance of being true to one's self that many people believe that being one's self and being selfish are the same thing. This belief manifests itself in many ways. Perhaps the most startling is the immediate assumption that a strong man who is "himself" is self-seeking and has the power to impose his will on others in order to get what he wants. This belief that the strong are selfish accounts for the attraction Ayn Rand's John Galt has for young people: they too would like to control others to get what they want.

Like Ayn Rand herself, many of her readers forget that men like Socrates, Christ, Buddha were not only themselves, they were also strong in ways that men like John Galt never dream of. Ayn Rand and her readers say they admire men like Galt because they do things, they act. But merely to act is hardly enough, we must consider the importance of a man's actions, and nothing is more important, I venture to say, than the influence a man's actions have on other men. Judged by this standard, how much influence does a man like Galt have on other men compared to the spiritual leaders I have named? I say nothing about *the kind* of influence men like Galt have had as compared to the others.

The truth of the matter is that people today are tragically confused about the self. Once more I turn to Erich Fromm's account of this confusion; Fromm makes the present situation marvellously clear. Fromm explains that we are taught that selfishness is a sin, but at the same time we live under an economic and political system which is based on the doctrine "that the most powerful and legitimate drive in man is selfishness and that by following this imperative drive the individual makes his best contribution to the common good." Fromm finds it "puzzling that two such contradictory principles could be taught side by side in one culture; of the fact, however, there is no doubt. One result of this contradiction is confusion in the individual. Torn between the two doctrines, he is seriously blocked in the process of integrating his personality. This confusion," Fromm concludes, "is one of the most significant sources of bewilderment and helplessness of modern man."

Fromm's explanation of the process whereby we are indoctrinated in the evils of selfishness reveals the root of our confusion. "The doctrine that selfishness is the arch-evil and that to love oneself excludes loving others is one of the stock ideas promulgated in home, school, motion pictures, books; indeed in all instruments of social suggestion as well. 'Don't be selfish' is a sentence which has been impressed upon millions of children, generation after generation. Its meaning is somewhat vague. Most people would say that it means not to be egotistical, inconsiderate, without any concern for others. Actually, it generally means more than that.

"Not to be selfish implies not to do what one wishes, to give up one's own wishes for the sake of those in authority. Aside from its obvious implications, 'don't be selfish' means 'don't love yourself,' 'don't be yourself,' but submit yourself to something more important than yourself, to an outside power or its internalization, 'duty.' 'Don't be selfish' becomes one of the most powerful ideological tools in suppressing spontaneity and the free development of personality. Under the pressure of this slogan one is asked for every sacrifice and for complete submission; only those acts are 'unselfish' which do not serve the individual but somebody or something outside himself." Most young people today are willing victims to this indoctrination.

Still young people will sometimes talk wistfully about being themselves, meaning the self-seeking of a John Galt. Here they reveal the other side of our attitude toward selfishness, our conviction that everyone will benefit if we all put self-interest before everything else. But they are no nearer to being themselves. Fromm says that if we really knew what our self-interest was this would work fine, but we don't. "Man has only one real interest, and that is the full development of his potentialities, of himself as a human being. Just as one has to know another person and his real needs in order to love him, one has to know one's own self in order to understand what the interests of this real self are and how they can be served." Whether we are being selfish or unselfish, in other words, we are confused because we simply do not know our true selves.

Fromm has touched here on the real problem of being true to one's self, and that is the discovery of the true self. Wilhelm Dilthey believed that "it is only in comparing myself with others that I come to experience what is individual in myself; only then do I become conscious of that in my own existence which differs from others, and Goethe is only too right in saying that this, the most important of all our experiences, is very difficult for us, and our insight into the extent, the nature, and the limits of our powers always remains very imperfect."

We can learn who and what we are by observing others, Dilthey says, but he looks to literature as the greatest source of self-knowledge. He believes that only in speech does the inner life of a man reveal itself, and literature is the most eloquent speech we have. It is natural for men to seek for a unity and a direction in their lives. "With most people," Dilthey says, "this happens occasionally and spasmodically, but with some it becomes their chief concern, they enquire systematically into the meaning of their own lives, and often give literary expression to what they find." In reading such a work of literature, we sometimes "understand more than we know," because inspired reading is an imaginative re-creation of the work, a reliving within ourselves of the life it expresses.

I agree with Dilthey that the study of literature is a very good way to gain self-knowledge. The simplest way in which we learn about ourselves through literature is by "identification," which is the feeling of close sympathy a reader has with an author or with a character in one of his stories. Like all subjective and emotional responses, this "identification" is frowned upon today by teachers of literature. But I know of no better way to discover who we are

70

and what kind of person we are meant to be. Merely the type of character we identify with reveals a great deal about us. And as the character we identify ourselves with goes through the experiences of the story, we learn through our sympathy, or antipathy, what we might have done in similar circumstances. In this way we learn something about ourselves, and also about how we ought to live.

If all this is true, then why do teachers of literature discourage "identification" and emotional responses to literature in their students? The reason, I suspect, is that they find their lives easier without the disrupting influence of strong feelings and beliefs in their students. I suppose that everything is easier for everyone this way, and we are a people who love comfort beyond anything else. There is less risk involved when students do not know who they are. To know who you are is "to venture wholly to be oneself, as an individual man, this definite individual man, alone in this tremendous responsibility," as Kierkegaard says. Is this what teachers want from their students? Is it what they want for themselves?

Just as I was finishing this book I came across an interesting passage in William Carlos Williams's *Paterson*: "Those very ideas and feelings which make one a writer with some kind of new vision are often the *very same ones* which, in living itself, make one clumsy, awkward, absurd, ungrateful, confidential where most people are reticent, and reticent where one should be confidential, and which cause one, all too often, to step on the toes of other people's sensitive egos as a result of one's stumbling earnestness or honesty carried too far. And that they *are* the very same ones — that's important, something to be remembered at all times, especially by people who are so sheltered from life in the raw by the glass-walled conditions of their own safe lives." Now I would say that these are the very things which are circumspectly avoided in the teaching of literature today. People in general simply do not like to be made uncomfortable, and teachers of literature are no different.

In *Walden,* Thoreau pokes fun at the man who "hastens to South Africa to chase giraffes. Surely that is not the game he would be after. How long, pray, would a man hunt giraffes if he could?

71

Snipes and woodcocks also may afford rare sport; but I trust it would be nobler game to shoot one's self." What he means is that it is harder to find out who we are than it is to hunt big game. It is more risky too: "It is easier to sail many thousand miles through cold and storm and cannibals, in a government ship, with five hundred men and boys to assist one, than it is to explore the private sea, the Atlantic and Pacific ocean of one's being," says Thoreau. If I find my real self, who knows what I might do? I see plenty of things going on around me that I would like to fight against if I only had the nerve. But people get killed this way, witness the integrationists in the South. Thoreau is right, it is easier to hunt giraffes.

Though all this seems perfectly clear to me, I am very well aware that not very many people today have a very good understanding of their selves, or even desire it. Perhaps this has always been the way things are, but I suspect that men today are subjected to a greater number of powerful forces of depersonalization than ever before. Because of this they have to overcome greater obstacles in getting to know their selves. Today we all feel powerless in the grip of events which involve millions of men, billions of dollars, and megatons of energy which we are at a loss to understand. The great conquests that man has made over nature, matter, space, and everything except himself, have emphasized our insignificance. Perhaps our deepest conviction is that our puny individual actions do not count for much.

Alexis de Tocqueville observed long ago that such a feeling was the natural result of democratic life. Though the citizen of a democracy is proud to feel the equal of any man, "when he comes to survey the totality of his fellows and to place himself in contrast with so huge a body, he is instantly overwhelmed by the sense of his own insignificance and weakness." This feeling of feebleness and helplessness in the face of overwhelming forces and numbers, I believe, lies at the root of the American impulse to conform to established social behavior. Men cannot long endure feelings of inadequacy and weakness, and by submerging themselves in the mass, even "the foolish, ignorant, and envious person is freed from the sense of his insignificance and worthlessness." So said Gustave Le Bon at the turn of the century, and subsequent books, Ortega y Gasset's *The Revolt of the Masses,* and Erich Fromm's *Escape from Freedom,* have made it clear that the willing surrender of individuality is perhaps the most widespread disorder afflicting our civilization.

In the United States today this willing surrender of individuality goes under the name of "conformity." Our tendency to conform has been given a great deal of attention of late; however, I do not believe that we have really gotten to the root of the matter, and I begin to wonder if we really want to. We have all been told again and again that the price of conformity is the loss of the deep satisfactions of being one's self, but it is obvious that people who conform do not feel this loss very much or they would not conform. As Kierkegaard pointed out, they are very contented to be in despair.

I cannot answer for people my own age, but I know that very few college students seem to have any notion whatever of the strength and happiness, the deep satisfactions I spoke of, which only true individuality can bring. True individuality to them is popping somebody in the nose when they feel like it. Now we are back to Ayn Rand's John Galt. In other words they have absolutely no notion of what it is to be a real person. Perhaps they will learn this in college, though I didn't; if not, unless life itself teaches them, they will never be aware that they have lost anything in their despair. As far as I can see they seem perfectly content to be "men of paper," carbon copies of everyone else, as Dostoevsky puts it.

To me the great risk of conformity is not the loss of individuality, grave as it is, but losing contact with one's true self. To put it quite simply, if I try too hard to be like everyone else, I may forget who I really am. In his essay "On Dissimulation," Sir Francis Bacon sets forth the advantages of conformity. As England's Lord Chancellor, the highest judge in England, Bacon himself was accused and convicted of taking bribes. Present-day scholars regard him as more unlucky than vicious, and excuse his conduct on the grounds that taking bribes was common practice in those days.

They are as bemused as Bacon. Have they no suspicion that not everyone stands to get by with "common practice"? What others may do with impunity may ruin me; it all depends on who I am. Bacon was a man many hated, feared, and envied. Did he dissimulate with himself so far as to forget that? If so, he was soon reminded of it. One marvels that he should be so much admired for playing Mephistopheles to his own Faust.

Whatever Bacon's reasons were, I think that men today take bribes of one kind or another simply because they cannot believe that their actions are significant enough to have social consequences. The only disadvantage they see is the punishment which society will inflict on them if they are caught. If they are not found out, they believe taking a little bribe or two really has no consequences. But when a man denies that his actions have consequences to society or to himself (unless he is punished for them), he denies his humanity and his bonds with other men. Like a machine or an animal he has no sense of responsibility because he has no awareness of self. This seems to me the most terrible punishment of all, and it is a punishment we all share. Dostoevsky's Father Zossimov taught that the guilt of the man who denies his humanity is binding upon us all; the whole of mankind is deprived when a man loses his self.

Were it not for our confusion about the nature of man, we would see clearly that any man who believes that being found out is the worst possible thing that can happen to him is making a tragic mistake. He forgets that loss of self-respect is often so much harder to bear than punishment that men willingly seek their punishment rather than bear their guilt. Henri Bergson explains that criminals do their utmost to conceal a crime not because they fear punishment so much, but because they want "to wipe out the past, to arrange things just as though the crime had not been committed at all."

It is the crime itself the criminal seeks to escape; like Lady Macbeth he wants to wash away the memory of it. But because he knows what he is and what he has done, the criminal feels he has cut himself off from society. Often this feeling of isolation is too much for him and the criminal will confess in an effort to rejoin society by taking his punishment. By doing this, Bergson says, the criminal "would be in a small degree the author of his own condemnation; and a part of himself, the best part, would thus escape punishment." Through retribution, then, the criminal becomes partly responsible for righting the wrong he has done and he thus regains his self-respect.

Dostoevsky has portrayed many such criminals, and they are among his greatest achievements as a novelist. *Crime and Punishment,* for example, is the story of a young intellectual, Raskolnikov, who commits two murders as an experiment "to prove he is not a louse like everyone else." Afterwards Raskolnikov finds himself in the position of a man condemned to death, content "to live on some high rock, on such a narrow ledge that he's only room to stand, and the ocean, everlasting darkness, everlasting solitude, everlasting tempest around him." This strikes me as a very good description of the criminal's feeling of isolation. Raskolnikov remains in this painful state until he is finally persuaded by Sonia, a saintly prostitute, to go to the police and give himself up.

In an epilogue, Dostoevsky tells of Raskolnikov's regeneration through the faith and love inspired in him by Sonia. Many readers today reject this epilogue (Ernest J. Simmons among them); they say it is artistically unconvincing. I suspect that what they really mean is they would feel more comfortable if Raskolnikov had shot himself, as Dostoevsky originally intended. Once Raskolnikov is dead they can forget him. Furthermore such readers refuse to believe that a murderer like Raskolnikov can be regenerated through suffering, which means that they do not believe in the regenerative power of suffering at all. Nothing I can think of reveals their moral and spiritual degeneracy more than this.

The story in *Crime and Punishment* is simple, but Dostoevsky's genius transforms it into an epic-tragedy of a human soul. I do not believe that there is a more painstaking, penetrating, and illuminating study of the torments of guilt in all literature. Next to the New Testament I know of nothing which offers greater proof of the divine in man than the resurrection of this warped young intellectual through his terrible ordeal of sin and suffering. In Raskolnikov Dostoevsky has given us the answer to the riddle of *Hamlet,* if we could but see it.

Raskolnikov deluded himself into thinking that he was a man like Napoleon, a man above the law of ordinary men; therefore he regarded his experiment in murder as an act of genius rather than a crime. But his experiment failed when his mind could not suppress his emotions of fear and repugnance; he could only be ruthless in theory. He could not accept his failure, however, because according to his theory this would have proved him beneath, rather than above, ordinary men; he could not accept his guilt either, because this would have made him a common criminal. Pride was his abiding sin: he refused to recognize his better self (he was by nature deeply, agonizingly compassionate) because he was convinced that power over others would make him strong.

Naturally his self-willed delusion that he was a superman brought about a conflict between his true self and the imaginary one he had created in his mind. His behavior became very erratic: he alternated between swaggering arrogance and cringing timidity, just like some present-day juvenile delinquents. Strangely enough his pseudo-self appeared to be the stronger of the two: even after he confessed he did not regret anything except that he had given himself up before it was absolutely necessary. It was only after he had been in prison and weakened by sickness that his true nature overcame his pride. When this happened, "everything, even his crime, his sentence and imprisonment, seemed to him now in the first rush of feeling an external, strange fact with which he had no concern." In other words, in regaining his true self, Raskolnikov repudiated the crimes he had committed in the guise of his pseudo-self.

The question is why did Raskolnikov suppress his true self in the first place? I believe he did this because like many of us he reasoned that senseless suffering is unjust. His compassion made him suffer through the misfortunes of others, misfortunes which he had nothing to do with and which he could do nothing about. He felt helpless in the face of human misery, and his intellect told him that this bond with suffering humanity was a source of weakness and needless suffering. As a consequence he turned his intellect against his emotions with the result that he suppressed his real self. In effect, Raskolnikov made his intellect the guiding force in his life. What he actually did was to destroy the best part of himself. Dostoevsky regarded the intellect, not the body or the emotions, as the diabolical part of man. Sonia told Raskolnikov the truth about himself: "You turned away from God, and God has smitten you, has given you over to the devil!"

Like us, Raskolnikov respected just one kind of power, brute force. What he wanted was power to dominate and control others, power over life and death, power to destroy. He hated Sonia's meekness and gentleness; he hated them because she was stronger in her helplessness than he was in his power-mad fantasies. In denying his own goodness, his compassion for others, Raskolnikov had gained only the power to hate and to destroy. Sonia's strength came from accepting in herself the very thing that Raskolnikov had rejected, compassion, and in the end she saved him because he could no longer save himself. He recognized bitterly that she was right when she told him that in his exultation over the power of life and death he had handed himself over to the Devil.

In our exultation over our own power to destroy, I wonder if we are not in the same pitiable situation as Raskolnikov? It seems strange to me that it should have taken me so long to learn that meekness and helplessness such as Sonia's, if they stem from love, are twice as strong as the Napoleonic power that Raskolnikov dreamed of. Like him, we are tragically confused about human values in regarding Sonia's gentle submissiveness as "weakness," and we do. The kind of power Sonia had cannot be measured in megatons of energy, but it alone can save mankind. Today the Biblical phrase, "the meek shall inherit the earth," means just what it says: when the power-mad get done with the human race, only the meek will be left.

Sonia can teach us something else: that we can only gain her kind of strength by being steadfastly faithful to our true selves. This was the source of her strength. She accepted her compassion and the great suffering that it brought, suffering that would have destroyed Raskolnikov, the would-be superman. So that her family might eat, she went into the street to offer herself to any degenerate brute who had money in his pocket. What this meant to a timid and sensitive girl such as Sonia could only be dimly imagined by Raskolnikov.

In some mysterious way Sonia was compensated for her suffering by a deepening of her religious faith, greatness of soul, and unfailing resiliency. Raskolnikov, who denied the good in himself, became a plagiarist without "a sign of independent life, a translation instead of an original," as his friend Razumihin said of him. As a consequence, Raskolnikov floundered in mental, emotional, and spiritual abjection. Through Sonia, who survives her ordeal and is purified and made strong and happy, Dostoevsky portrays his belief in the necessity of sin and suffering. But most of us are like Raskolnikov, who, in the pride of his will to power, became weak and miserable, as worthless to himself as to others. We do not believe in the necessity of sin and suffering any more than Raskolnikov did, and we are paying for it with the same meagerness of soul.

In this story Dostoevsky also expresses his belief that every man has within him a potentiality for bringing some unique good into the world. I agree wholeheartedly with this. The unique good in each of us, I believe, is what men are referring to when they speak of God, or perhaps God is all the good in all men put together. However, that thought is not essential to my theology, if I may call it that. What is essential is that each man has a bit of divinity in him. This I believe to be his true self. What he must do to gain salvation, to become strong like Sonia, is to discover and to become this good as much as he can. Christ, who had a great deal more good in him than most of us, became this good completely, and so we call him God. He set an example which most of us find very difficult to follow; nevertheless it is our duty to do our best "to enter into the Kingdom of Heaven within us," as Christ himself said. We will never get anywhere if, like Ibsen's Peer Gynt, we complain that the task is too difficult. It was stupid of Peer to expect that it would be easy, and we are no different.

I believe that those who fail to discover the good, or, having found it, haven't the strength to become it, are the great majority of mankind to which I belong. Dante, who put people like me in the ante-room of his Inferno, called us "the Trimmers," and said of us, "They lived without blame, and without praise, but were for themselves. Those who have no hope of death because they were never really alive: and whose blind life is so mean that they are envious of every other lot, those who could not even enter hell because the damned would have some glory over them." In contrast to these "Trimmers," those who find the good in themselves and become it to a marked degree, like Sonia, are saints; those who find it and deny it to a marked degree are the great sinners, like Raskolnikov.

Denial of the good in oneself is, to me, the only true sin, and anything which tempts us to it is evil; or, to use an old-fashioned image, the devil. As Mephistopheles says himself, "I am the spirit which denies." Raskolnikov's devil was his intellect. Dostoevsky regarded science, the intellect in its highest perfection, as a force which would tempt modern man to place himself in the bondage of death and destruction. Raskolnikov's fall, therefore, is symbolic of our own; although there are still people who deny that we have fallen, despite Hitler's ovens and the two hells our nuclear physicists created over Japan.

Such thoughts as these explain why I regard the discovery of the good in us, our true selves, as a matter of ultimate concern. I do not regard my "theological" notions as essential to this discovery. At best I regard them as merely a translation of basic Christian concepts, a translation which I am forced to make because the way these concepts are interpreted in churches today, and the language these interpretations are expressed in, are as meaningless to me as they were to Kierkegaard a century ago. I do not want anyone to feel, however, that because I do not attach a great deal of importance to my theology, except for myself, that they needn't concern themselves about the main point of it. On the contrary, the works of Spinoza, Goethe, Kierkegaard, Dostoevsky and a great many deep students of man have convinced me that discovering the true self, and accepting the obligations this discovery places on us, is the main business of life.

CHAPTER VII

FINDING ONE'S TRUE SELF

At this point I believe it would be well for me to answer, as best I can, those questions and objections which are sure to arise when I advocate a personal approach to the study of literature. Since we are all different, when a work of literature is studied with the end of finding out who and what we are, and how we ought to live, we will all come away with a different answer. If we proceed in this way, what possible chance have we of establishing and maintaining an objectively valid literary criticism? In the preceding chapters I have also laid great stress on the importance of finding one's true self, and on the strength which becoming a true individual alone can bring. What proof is there that this "true self" actually exists; what proof is there that we have power to choose it supposing that it does exist; and what proof is there that in finding and choosing our true selves we become strong?

The limitations of a personal approach to literature are so obvious I could not ignore them even if I wanted to. For example, there is the ever-present danger of forcing everything one reads to mean what one wants it to mean; in other words, to read in the light of one's reflected ego, according to one's emotional needs, one's prejudices, one's preconceptions. Certainly nothing is more deplorable than this, nothing more likely to prevent personal growth. But do the limitations of the personal approach mean that the impersonal approach has none? I believe that it has a great many. It seems to me, in fact, that the ideal of an impersonal literary criticism is precisely what is wrong with the study of literature today: by depersonalizing the study of literature we have deprived it of all life. We have tried to make over the study of literature in the image of the sciences — cold, calculating, detached, unfeeling, objective. But instead of making it impersonal, we have killed it.

How can the study of literature avoid the personal element when each of us is bound to have a somewhat different understanding of what we read? Every reader has varying powers of comprehension. We can do absolutely nothing about these differences since they depend on a reader's intelligence, his experience with literature in general, with similar works by the same author, and so on. Upon this unalterable difference are superimposed such things as social or religious prejudices, differences in sex, adherence to different critical theories, to say nothing of the differences in geographical and cultural situations in which a work is read. It may sound idiotic to those who have not experienced reading the same book in different places, but I found out in reading Dickens that his stories are one thing if you read them in San Francisco, and something quite different when you read them in London where a lot of his characters still walk the streets.

Perhaps some unusual readers are capable of overcoming one or two of these differences which tend to make the same book appear to be one thing to an American, another to an Englishman, still another to a Frenchman, but certainly they cannot overcome them all. Even if they could, I question whether it would be worth the trouble. A completely depersonalized literary criticism, it seems to me, would have to be based on precisely those elements of literature which can best be analyzed, tabulated, and totalled up by an IBM machine. The fact that this tabulating-machine criticism is actually being used at Harvard and the University of California, from where it will doubtless spread all over the country, is an indication of how deeply some teachers of literature distrust subjectivity.

I do not mean that statistical studies of literature are worthless: they are as valuable as the textual, historical, sociological, psychological, esthetic, or comparative studies, all of which have proven their usefulness. There is a place for all; all contribute to our knowl-

81

edge and understanding of literature. In the end, however, we reach the fullest understanding of a work of literature in our personal experience with it, an experience in which we assimilate all of the knowledge offered by such studies. Personal experience with a work of literature is necessary, as Wilhelm Dilthey explains, because the act of reading is in part an imaginative re-creation of what is read, and this imaginative re-creation enables us to project our self into the other self of the author to a greater or lesser degree. Dilthey describes this imaginative act, as well he might, as "divination." It often leads to results which cannot be demonstrated, hence such results are suspect in the eyes of logical-minded people; nevertheless these results are sometimes more important to a perceptive reader than those offered by systematic research or an IBM machine.

In my view, anyone who finds it impossible to divine more from a work of literature than can be demonstrated by logic, sees no more than appears on the page: for him the author's whole intent is in the words themselves, and he feels that the words are all he can know and needs to know. Kazantsakis says of words that "they are the black bars of the prison where the spirit strangles itself with screaming. Between the letters and the lines, and all around the blank margins, the spirit circulates freely." In order to contact this spirit we have to put ourselves in the position of a sympathetic listener who is more intent on grasping what a speaker means than what he is actually saying. A great many literal-minded people regard this haphazard process as hopeless, but in plain truth it is the human way of doing things. As most of us are aware, our own endeavours to put thoughts and feelings into words have only approximate results, and we are also aware that a sympathetic listener will often understand far more than our mere words express. Therefore when we ourselves are in sympathy with an author we should not be surprised to discover that we can do the same thing.

My own attempts to write have taught me that writing is often a very imperfect expression of what I mean to say. Sometimes the words I have to use prove intractable: they do not convey the precise idea I have in my head. Often the effort to present thoughts in an interesting way, with due proportion and emphasis, will clarify my thoughts; but just as often these requirements prevent me from giving the fullest expression to my ideas. I have learned that if you flog a reader with an idea he will not understand you better, he will merely yawn. Furthermore, when a writer has finished a book, does his thinking stop there? On the contrary, isn't it true that in the process of writing we generate new thoughts, and that when we have finished writing there is still something left unsaid?

We tend to assume that everything can be expressed by a skillful writer, but can it? When King Dionysius wrote to Plato requesting a short and simple explanation of his philosophy, Plato replied — with some pique I expect — that his philosophy never had been and never could be reduced to writing. "The sole way of acquiring it," he wrote, "is by strenuous intellectual communion and intimate personal intercourse." In other words Plato felt that certain aspects of his teaching could only be transmitted through personal associations. Others have said the same thing: Sir Rabindranth Tagore observes about Buddha's teachings "that those who listened to the great teacher did not merely hear his words and understand his doctrines, they directly felt in him what he was preaching, in the living language of his person, the ultimate truth of man."

I can readily believe that the fullest understanding of the great teachings of such men as Plato, Buddha, Christ, Mohammed, are to be gained only through knowing the men themselves. Such men were artists at life; in the fullest sense their lives were artistic creations which could not be described in words. In order to fully understand such men we would have to know them personally. We would have to know them personally for the same reason we must experience a work of literature for ourselves, so that we can make an imaginative re-creation of their experiences in ourselves. Lacking this personal contact, as we do, we have to do the best we can with accounts of these intimate personal teachings by men who knew them.

The reason I have brought all this up is that the most convincing evidence I have found for the existence of a "true self" in man is of a similar nature. I do not believe that I or anyone else can logically demonstrate that deep within us we have a hidden self which I think of as the potentiality of the unique person that we were meant to be. A student of the works of Dostoevsky, Vyacheslav Ivanov, holds that this hidden self is a matter of pure belief. He maintains that the question of faith is no longer, "Do you believe in God?", but, "Do you believe in your Ego, that it truly exists, that it transcends your ephemerality and darkness and is greater than you in your impotence and littleness?"

If a person answers "no" to this question, what proofs will convince him? Obviously none will. In matters of faith, arguments are only convincing if one already partly believes. The best that I can do, then, is to present evidence for the true self which I found convincing at a time when I already half believed. Of the two forms in which the evidence came to me, the biographical and the philosophical, I found the biographical the most instructive, and therefore I will present it first.

I think that the best description I have ever read of a man's discovery of his true self is John Middleton Murry's. In *Things to Come,* Murry tells how the death of his wife, Katherine Mansfield, and the simultaneous failure of all his hopes as a writer, reduced him to the point where his life meant so little to him that he ceased to care what happened next. At this point, Murry says, a surprising thing happened: he discovered in himself some ultimate principle of being which gave him absolute faith in himself and in life. From that moment on, he says, he knew with absolute certainty that nothing life offered could ever faze him again. Just when it seemed to him that his life was not even worth throwing away, he found that it gained its greatest value; in the depths of utter hopelessness he found an inviolability of spirit.

Henry Miller has given us a similar description of discovering his true self at the moment of utter failure: the moment when, in his own words, "I was nothing — less than nothing — a minus quantity." Miller tells how he failed in everything men regard as important, his job, his marriage, his duties as a father. Moreover he knew he had failed as a writer, and to him this was the greatest failure of all. He felt that he had been born to write; to fail as a writer meant to fail utterly.

Looking back, Miller saw that his failure was necessary. "I had to grow foul with knowledge," he writes, "realize the futility of everything; smash everything, grow desperate, then humble, then sponge myself off the slate as it were, in order to recover my authenticity." It was then that he found himself as a writer. He heard his first original word. "Immediately I heard my own voice, I was enchanted: the fact that it was a separate, distinct, unique voice sustained me. It didn't matter to me if what I wrote should be considered bad. I had found a voice, I was whole again." Like Murry, Miller found that at the moment when his life seemed utterly wasted, he came face to face with his ultimate self, a self which gave him the strength, the courage, the originality and the vitality which are so unmistakable in his writing.

It seems to me that in losing everything most men set their hearts on, success, fame, power, money, the love of women, all the things which tempt men to deny their true selves, both Miller and Murry were left one final, desperate choice, to become their true selves, and they took it.

Arthur Miller, the playwright, has given dramatic treatment to the same kind of choice in *The Crucible,* the title of which suggests the ordeal his hero goes through. Miller's hero, John Proctor, ends up in the hands of the Puritan inquisitors who threaten to kill him unless he signs his name to a "confession" which will incriminate a number of his friends. Though his own life is at stake, Proctor finds that he cannot let his name be used to betray his friends. The reasons he gives are not very rational, but perhaps they are all the better for that. The only reasonable thing to do would have been to sign. But Proctor finds he cannot surrender his name, "Because it is my name! Because I cannot have another in my life! How may I live without my name?" After he decides not to sign, Proctor goes calmly to the gallows convinced at last that there is "some shred of goodness in John Proctor." Like Henry Miller and Middleton Murry, John Proctor found that his desperate choice brought him an inviolability of spirit, that he had found his life in losing it.

I do not know how many men are capable of making this kind of choice. Not many I expect. I have serious doubts about myself, for one. But the point here is not the ease or practicality of choosing to be one's true self, but of convincing oneself that the possibility of such a choice actually exists. One of the worst evils of our time is that the more deeply learned a man becomes, the less he is inclined to grant man a true self, a self of which science knows nothing and does not care to know. The other day I was talking with an engineer friend of mine about a saying of Rousseau's to the effect that if you deny freedom of choice to a man, you demoralize him. "Do you agree with this?" I asked. He did. "Many psychologists," I said, "deny it. Are they deliberately trying to demoralize us?" No, he didn't think so. "How do you explain their denial, then?" "They are either very stupid," he said, "or very ignorant of what it means to be human."

What my friend said may be closer to the truth than either of us realized at the time. Jules Henry says about the same thing in a recent review of a new book, *Human Behavior*, a sort of encyclopedia of the social sciences. "All the apparent errors of judgment in the social sciences," he writes, "derive from the fact that they avoid human existence." Then he goes on to quote the editors of this book, who sum up their work this way: "As one reviews this set of findings, he may well be impressed by a striking omission. As one lives life or observes it around him (or within himself) or finds it in a work of art, he sees a richness that somehow has fallen through the present screen of the behavioral sciences. This book, for example, has rather little to say about central human concerns: nobility, moral courage, ethical torment, the delicate relation of father and son or of the marriage state, life's way of corrupting innocence, the rightness and wrongness of acts, evil, happiness, love and death, hate, even sex." I do not know how others may feel, but I find this admission as damning as it is candid.

But the question of man's freedom of choice, which has perplexed Western man more, and for a longer period, than any other, is far from simple. In contrast to the success man has had in probing nature's secrets, his own nature has become more of a puzzle than ever. The thoughts of countless artists, philosophers, scientists, and writers of all kinds have simply added to the confusion. After twenty years and more of bewilderment, I have come to the conclusion that we never will see any agreement on this question.

Curiously enough, this very lack of agreement forces each of us to decide for himself whether he believes he is free or bound. Determinists will argue, of course, that even this choice is decided for us. They may be right. As for myself, I believe that I do have the freedom to choose in the matter. My "freedom," however, is a human freedom; and as such it is subject to all the limitations which are an inseparable part of human existence. In no sense of the word do I feel that I have absolute freedom to do as I please, which is what most people seem to think you mean when you say that you are free.

A great deal of misunderstanding has been created, I believe, by this tendency on both sides to insist that if man is free he must be absolutely free; free, that is, to do anything he likes. But man, who must exist in a given time and place, cannot possibly be free in this way. I am not free, for example, to choose to be a Roman emperor; nor can I choose to become the first man to climb Everest; no more can I become a mother, my sex forbids it. If I am free, then, it must be a limited human freedom. Erich Fromm explains this better than I can. He says that man's freedom is not a "freedom to," but a "freedom from." What Fromm means is that although I am not free to do anything that comes into my head, I am by no means bound, as animals are, by instinct, training, and impulse. Embarked upon one course of action, I am free to change it for another whenever I see fit.

For example, faced with a choice of believing whether man is bound by nature, or free, I feel that I am free to choose (within narrow limits) what I am to believe, and I will continue to believe this until something or someone persuades me to change it for another. The limits within which my choice must take place are determined, for example, by the fact that I have to understand the problem as well as my limited human mind permits. Being human, I must do the best I can with approximations: such things as certainty and complete knowledge are denied to me. Furthermore, if I choose to believe that man is free, I must do so in spite of the fact that I am mistaken insofar as man is determined. What becomes most important to me, then, is not that man is always free to choose, but sometimes free, or even once in a lifetime free.

Convinced of that, I choose to believe in the rest. I am certain that no self-respecting determinist will accept this kind of argument, but has he not done exactly the same thing himself? But it would be very difficult to get such an admission out of a determinist, because insofar as he is willing to admit that he too has chosen what to believe, he admits that he has committed a free human act. As a matter of fact if we admit for one moment that P. W. Bridgman is right in insisting that all knowledge, scientific knowledge above all, is subjective, then a determinist simply cannot deny his choice without discrediting his science.

I see, however, that in trying to explain these conclusions of mine I am in some danger of becoming dogmatic, and nothing is further from my wish. Apparently there is something about this question of man's freedom which leads to polemics. Perhaps this is because our emotions are involved. I freely admit that I yearn to believe that man is free; is there a determinist in the house who will stand up and admit that he yearns just as strongly, even more strongly in my opinion, to deny man his freedom? I feel that many a misunderstanding would be cleared up if we could only bring ourselves to admit to our true feelings. We are only men after all.

To me the question is far too important for ill-will, stubbornness, and perversity to enter into it. If it is really true that a man's happiness depends upon his choosing to become his true self, we certainly ought to exercise the greatest patience, tolerance, and readiness to understand the opposite point of view before we decide whether or not we are going to believe that man is free to make such an important choice, or deny him this freedom. Irritability and intolerance are serious handicaps for anyone who is really searching for the truth. I learned this when I first looked into the work of Spinoza.

I admire and respect Spinoza as a philosopher. He does not philosophize merely for the sake of making theories. Like the present-day existentialists he tries to figure out the best way for a man to live. If you want answers to the countless epistemological and ontological puzzles which perplex philosophers, he can't help you. But if you want to know how to live a better life, Spinoza is your man. Because I am very sympathetic to Spinoza's ideas, I was very disappointed when I discovered that Spinoza denies man any semblance of freedom of choice. By the time I made this discovery, however, all I could think of was doing my best not to misunderstand or undervalue what he was trying to teach me. For the first time I realized that perhaps not all determinists belong to the devil's party.

Spinoza holds that God is the universe, the universe God, and that all things, man included, are manifestations of eternal natural forces which he refers to, in theological language, as "God's will." According to Spinoza, all things in the universe are as they must be because they could not possibly be any different than they are. This applies also to man; each of us is as we must be, our freedom is an illusion. In every situation we act according to our given natures, because we cannot do otherwise. Since we are exactly as we must be, we deserve neither praise nor blame; each of us is perfect in his own way, even the homicidal maniac. Spinoza admits that the homicidal maniac must be destroyed, but we do this to protect ourselves, not because of his "imperfection." In other words, Spinoza's view of man seems to be exactly that of present-day psychological determinists.

It seems to me, however, that Spinoza's determinism ranges far beyond the narrow limits of those determinists who believe that men always act out of necessity. For example, Spinoza advances the idea that a man ought to live in accordance with moral principles, and that these principles properly arise out of his innermost character and constitution; they are not derived from any external authority which he can expect either to reward or to punish him in accordance with his true deserts. According to Spinoza, we act morally insofar as we act in accordance with our own natures.

Leon Roth says that Spinoza's "main contention is that the man whose self is most real, whose eternal individuality is most concrete and valuable, is he whose life is one unswerving effort toward clear knowledge — not the knowledge of mere theory, but the knowledge which informs and vitalizes conduct." Such knowledge gives a man "an infinite enjoyment of being which makes him feel and experience that he is eternal." This sounds very much like Spinoza is saying that being one's self brings the greatest happiness, the thing I have been saying over and over. Kierkegaard and Dostoevsky both said much the same thing as Spinoza. If this is what present-day determinists believe, I can only applaud; but I doubt very much if they have the slightest notion of what Spinoza, Kierkegaard, and Dostoevsky are talking about.

But I am getting angry again, and my anger is not justified. I have to admit that I have never the courage to face the difficulties of being my true self, though I believe that such a self exists. I am not one of those men whose self is most real, whose eternal individuality is most concrete and valuable, though I would like to be were it not for the difficulties I mentioned. These difficulties have led me, like most men, to accept the sickness unto death which is despair. Nonetheless I am not mean enough to say that no man can be his true self, to deny the freedom of this choice to all men because I haven't the guts to make it.

I know from history that a few superhumans, Socrates, Christ, Buddha, became god-like through being their true selves. In our own time, too, John Middleton Murry and Henry Miller, and surely many others that I have not heard about, have testified to the exrtaordinary strength which came to them when they found the courage to throw off their despair. When I think of the agony they went through before this choice became possible, I blame no one, not even myself, for his reluctance to venture forth on a journey of discovery of his true self, a lonely and perilous journey of tremendous exertion and tremendous responsibility. But how I wish I had the courage.

CHAPTER VIII

RECOMMENDATIONS TO STUDENTS AND TEACHERS

I have tried to be honest throughout this book, and I will try to be honest still. The book I set out to write is finished. This chapter is tacked on at my wife's suggestion. She reminded me that it is not enough to criticize, I should offer solutions for some of the things I have complained about.

The trouble is I can't believe my solutions are going to be very helpful to anyone. There is no one best method of learning and teaching — each of us has to discover his own. Temperament dictates which method is best. People in education, like most Americans, have too simple and naïve a faith in method. Changes in method are not going to improve things, at least not in the teaching of literature.

I hadn't tried to teach very many literature courses before I realized that the basic problem I had to solve was not proper method, but to convince my students that literature really matters. From first to last, few are ever convinced that their knowledge of literature is anything more than a means of making a living or a social ornament, something to parade in chit-chat at cocktail parties. I am in favor of anything that will disabuse them of this notion. In this chapter I have set down some of the things that have been useful to me.

One of these is the discussion method. I think that the students should do most of the talking. After all it is *their* education they came for, isn't it? The older I get the more unhappy I become when I am facing a roomful of silent students. I am most happy sitting around a table listening to them exchange their ideas. (It is symptomatic of the present state of things that there is no such table in my department.) Student discussions are not great, few discussions are.[1] Nevertheless I am convinced that in their discussions the educational process is being carried out where it should be, in the minds of the students.

The sessions I like best are those which consist of questions and answers, where anyone can ask questions, but only the students can give answers. When they go astray I try to think of a question which will reveal the inadequacy of what has been said. I do not often succeed, but when I do the results fully justify the effort. When a student discovers for himself where he has gone wrong, he learns a great deal more than if he is merely corrected.

My conscience used to bother me a little about discussion classes. They are aimless and formless, and so they ought to be. Elaborate preparations and specific intent are desirable in most other ways of teaching, but you can't rig a free discussion. This lack of premeditation makes discussions more difficult to conduct than lectures, at least that is my experience. I notice that I do most of the talking when I am tired. Apparently I exert myself less when I am relaying information than I do when I am asking questions.

It may be elementary, but I would like to point out that an exchange of interpretations of a story, play, or poem is not necessarily an argument. I have what I feel to be a good interpretation; if you can persuade me that yours, or a part of it, is better than mine, I will modify mine or exchange it for yours. In this way I finally arrive at what I feel is the "best" interpretation. Critics can be helpful in this process, providing we do not regard them as authoritative experts. I believe that students should arrive at their "best" interpretations in the same way. They are much better off with their own "best" interpretation than with any I can give them.

1. I cannot resist mentioning that my only discussion group which was an absolute failure was composed of teachers. The idea of this group was that we should all read books outside our specialities and come together to discuss them. The reason the group failed was simple: the teachers wouldn't read the books.

I used to believe my responsibility as a teacher was to gather the best criticism available and relay it to my students. Most teachers I know seem to have this idea. For one thing their students encourage it. I now have serious doubts. I have before me a talk which P. J. Rempel gave before the National Conference on Aims of Education in 1961. Rempel complains that "we regard the question as something to be abolished by an answer, and even more often, particularly in formal education, we busy ourselves with the task of supplying answers before questions are asked." As a result of this, "we no longer ask questions, we wait until someone comes along with the answers." Rempel asks what kind of citizens we are turning out if we lead them to always expect experts to feed them the answers. That's a good question.

Rempel believes that students and teachers must deal with some questions which have no final and complete answers. I could not agree more: it is the only way to keep one's curiosity alive. Teachers tend to forget that a student who is given "the answer" need not search any longer, nor need he take any further interest in the question. In fact, if he is given "the answer" to a question he has never asked, he doesn't even know what the question is.

The biggest objection to the discussion method is the quality of the discussions themselves. Most of my colleagues would be shocked if they overheard one of the discussions I have with students, and they would be right. Judged by the professional standards of specialists in the teaching of literature, they are hopeless. But if I am permitted to judge them on a much broader basis, on the basis, say, of development of the mind and personality of the student, these discussions affect students in ways that lectures never can. The students themselves recognize this. I have learned over the years that students in my discussion groups do not make as good a showing in examinations as those prepared by lectures. The students know the reason — examinations are judged by the same standards as prevail in the lectures — but they still want discussions rather than lectures. Teachers often forget how much of a student's time is spent sitting in lecture halls being jawed at.

While it is true that many of the things students say in discussions are not worth listening to, my lectures are no different. About half the ideas I carry around with me are junk, perhaps even more than half. I suspect other teachers are about the same. From the human point of view this intellectual junk may even be necessary. One of Doestoevsky's characters (Razumihin in *Crime and Punishment*) says that a man must think a thousand foolish and stupid thoughts before he thinks one good and true one. That has certainly been true for me. Have we a right to expect anything different from students? They must learn to crawl before they can climb.

The discussion method I am so fond of has at least one other advantage, it avoids the worst excesses of professionalism, specialization, and the historical point of view.

The other day at a meeting of teachers of literature I raised a big laugh when I said that Nabokov's *Pale Fire* did not interest me because I didn't learn anything from it. I was serious enough, and so were they, I expect. The highest praise I can give a book is to say that it taught me a great deal. Many teachers of literature, I. A. Richards is a good example, apparently believe that learning *about* literature is far more important than learning *from* it. This belief is consistent with their habit of looking at literature from the historical point of view.

In one of the Screwtape letters, C. S. Lewis explains why the Devil need have no fear of the wisdom in old books. "Only the learned read old books, and we have now so dealt with the learned that they are of all men the least likely to acquire wisdom by doing so. We have done this by inculcating the Historical Point of View. The Historical Point of View," Lewis explains, "means that when a learned man is presented with any statement in an ancient author, the one question he never asks is whether it is true. He asks who influenced the ancient writer, and how far the statement is consistent with what he said in other books, and what phase in the writer's development, or in the general history of thought, it illustrates, and how it affected later writers, and how often it has been misunderstood (especially by the learned man's own colleagues) and what the general course of criticism on it has been for

94

the last ten years, and what is the 'present state of the question.' To regard the ancient writer as a possible source of knowledge — to anticipate that what he said could possibly modify your thoughts or your behavior — this would be rejected as unutterably simple-minded."

Students also have a way of giving things the historical treatment if you let them. Confronted with reading matter which is in any way disturbing or unpleasant, let it be no more than a few years old and they will argue that it no longer applies, it is out of date. "That was long ago," they say. "Or perhaps not so long really," this when you point out that the number of years is small, "but progress is progressing faster all the time, and things are quite different now."

Once I insisted that they get specific and not fob me off with that rattle about progress. I pointed out that when I was their age the world looked much the same as it does now. "The only difference I can see," I said, "is television and space travel. As for space travel, I only see it on television. And television being what it is, I don't see how you can say that my world twenty-five years ago was very different from yours. At this point the conversation took a wild lurch. "It's not the world that's changed," said a girl student earnestly, "it's the *people*." That rocked me I can tell you. Before I could recover, the bell rang and I never did get to the bottom of it. I came away from that discussion more convinced than ever that I hadn't the vaguest notion of what was going on in their minds.

Now I want to turn my attention to professionalism and specialization, of which I have had much to say already. I know teachers who have turned themselves over body and soul to a professional speciality; they make a frightening spectacle. I was talking to one of them the other day about specialization. "Insofar as a man is a specialist," I said, "he is that much less human." "Whatever that means," he said. "To be human," I went on, "is to be many-sided, diverse, all over the place. A specialist takes all of this splendid multiplicity and directs it into one narrow groove." "I don't see anything wrong with that," he said. *"One* thing wrong with it," I said, "is that I have just had to explain to you what it is to be human." I must say he took it very well. The cream of the jest is this: he was an anthropologist; that is, a specialist in the science devoted to the study of man himself.

What upsets me the most when I am dealing with the out-and-out specialist is that he never seems to question the fundamental assumptions of his speciality. Perhaps the basis of many specializations will not bear scrutiny, the humanities for one. John Stuart Mill said of such men that "their conclusions may be true, but they might be false for anything they know: they have never thrown themselves into the mental position of those who think differently from them, and considered what such persons may have to say; and consequently they do not, in any proper sense of the word, know what they themselves profess."

Now the irony of all this is that I am a specialist myself and I don't suppose I would abolish specialization if I could. Specialists get things done. But they have got to realize that their specialization, which is their great strength, is also their great weakness. Somehow they have got to get outside their specializations, "to throw themselves into the mental position of those who think differently from them." I believe it is possible, if we are willing to give as much respect to specialists in other disciplines as we do to our own, to learn much from studying their shortcomings. I repeat, this study must be carried out with *respect*: the usual interdepartmental squabbles, the chest-beating, the crowing, the fund-snatching, and the exchanges of brickbats will not serve. Respect is essential because once we see the mote in the other fellow's eye, we must turn the same critical scrutiny on ourselves and respectfully seek out our own shortcomings.

I have said that teachers cannot surrender themselves to their specialities without loss, no more can students surrender themselves to their teachers. Far too many students come to college convinced that their best chance for success in the world (the all-important thing) is to surrender themselves mind, soul, and body to the educational process. On top of this, many students yearn for the security of an authoritarian relationship with their teachers. Teachers must not yield to this yearning. Students must be encouraged to maintain a sense of personal integrity and continuity of self; they must not be permitted to become passive objects to be manipulated and acted upon. Education involves interaction, otherwise it is mere brainwashing.

I know perfectly well that nine tenths of college work will still be devoted to turning out specialists. We've got to have specialists to keep things going. But I am talking about the education of a man, not the training of a socially useful human being. Therefore the remaining one tenth is what interests me, for this is where literature lives, or should live. Here there is no need to ram gobs of information down the student's throat. He is not being prepared to take his place as a cog or wheel in our industrial social machinery, but as a human being. Here the student should be allowed to take only what he finds useful to him as a human being, and he should let the rest alone.

This means that teachers of literature have got to revive their respect for subjectivity in dealing with students. The sciences are far advanced in this revival already, as Percy Bridgman makes clear in his introduction to *The Way Things Are*. Another fine and useful book in this regard is Phillip Frank's *Modern Science and Its Philosophy*, which I believe would inspire a great many teachers of literature to drop their old-fashioned notions of scientific objectivity. What teachers should aim for, I believe, is some sort of balance between subjectivity and objectivity; there exists no such balance in education today. Perhaps one way to do this is to give more encouragement to students to trust in their own reactions, to respect their own thoughts, and to express both clearly, simply, straightforwardly, and with vigor. I fail to see why students should be expected to write like contributors to the scholarly quarterlies. In fact the last thing they should be permitted to do is to ape the academic style. Few teachers express themselves well, teachers of literature included. I know because I am one of them.

Students should also be encouraged to write and speak in the first person when the first person is appropriate. Too many teachers still assume that we are all supposed to think as impersonally as IBM machines. This assumption, to my mind, is responsible for much of the gutlessness of academic writing. A character in Lawrence Durrell's *Black Book* says of some articles he has just read in a literary magazine, "These couldn't have been written by men, but by plants!" When the editor defends his writers, muttering something about their "palpable literary ability," his critic shouts at him, "It's not their ability one questions for a moment, it's their existence!"

Fundamentally, I believe, it is the cultivation of dispassionate disinterestedness in education which is cutting the ground from under our feet. I have observed in myself a tendency to defend only those ideas which mean something to me personally, ideas I feel strongly about. I will not give them up easily. But the ones I am indifferent about I am quite ready to change; here I can be serenely objective. But turn that around and you will see that if I am objective about all my ideas, I am indifferent about all. Any education which makes a man indifferent about his ideas is not worthy of the name.

The most important thing we have to do is to get rid of our distrust of our emotions. Far too many students regard ideas as objects which they push around in their minds, and we encourage them too much in this. Common expressions such as "love of truth," "love of beauty," "hatred of ugliness," "thirst for learning," and "hunger for knowledge" reveal the emotional and even the physical nature of our thought processes. If we can manage somehow to revive thought as a passion or an appetite of the mind, we will have done much to revitalize ideas as living matters of ultimate concern, instead of the lifeless objects we have made of them.

BIBLIOGRAPHY

Note: The books below, with the exception of those I have marked with an asterisk, are paperbound editions.

Henry Adams. *The Degradation of Democratic Dogma.* Introduction by Brooks Adams. N.Y.: Putnam Sons, Capricorn Books, 1958.

William Barrett. *Irrational Man.* Garden City, N.Y.: Doubleday Anchor Books, 1962.

*Henri Bergson. *Creative Evolution.* N.Y.: H. Holt and Co., 1911.

P. W. Bridgman. *The Way Things Are.* N.Y.: Viking Press Inc., 1961 .

Jacob Burckhardt. *Force and Freedom.* Boston: Beacon Press, 1964.

Dostoevsky. *The Brothers Karamazov.* 2 vols. Baltimore, Maryland: Penguin Books, 1951.

—— *Crime and Punishment.* Baltimore, Maryland: Penguin Books, 1951.

—— *The Idiot.* Baltimore, Maryland: Penguin Books, 1955.

—— *The Insulted and the Injured.* N.Y.: Grove Press, 1955.

—— *Notes from Underground.* N.Y.: E. P. Dutton, 1960.

—— *The Possessed.* N.Y.: Dell Publishing Co., 1956.

—— *A Raw Youth.* N.Y.: Dell Publishing Co., 1956.

Phillip Frank. *Modern Science and Its Philosophy.* N.Y.: Collier Books, 1961.

*Waldo Frank. *The Rediscovery of America.* N.Y.: C. Scribner's Sons, 1929.

Sigmund Freud. *Civilization and Its Discontents.* N.Y.: Norton, 1961.

*Erich Fromm. *The Escape from Freedom.* N.Y.: Farrar and Rinehart Inc., 1941.

*—— *Man for Himself.* N.Y.: Rinehart, 1947.

*H. W. Garrod. *Poetry and the Criticism of Life.* Cambridge: Harvard University Press, 1931.

Ortega y Gasset. *The Dehumanization of Art.* N.Y.: Doubleday and Co., Anchor Books, 1956.

—— *The Revolt of the Masses.* N.Y.: W. W. Norton and Co., 1964.

*C. Virgil Gheorghiu. *The 25th Hour.* N.Y.: Alfred A. Knopf, 1950.

André Gide. *Dostoevsky.* N.Y.: New Directions, 1961.

Goethe. *Faust.* Translated by B. Q. Morgan. N.Y.: Liberal Arts Press, Bobbs-Merrill Inc., 1957.

*Herbert Hodges. *Wilhelm Dilthey: An Introduction.* London: K. Paul, Trench, Trubner and Co., 1944.

William Hubben. *Four Prophets of Our Destiny: Kierkegaard, Dostoevsky, Nietzsche, Kafka.* N.Y.: Collier Books, 1962.

*Werner Jaeger. *Paideia: The Ideals of Greek Culture.* N.Y.: Oxford University Press, 1939.

*Franz Kafka. *The Trial.* N.Y.: Alfred A. Knopf, 1959.

Soren Kierkegaard. *The Present Age.* N.Y.: Harper and Row, 1962.

—— *Sickness Unto Death.* Garden City, N.Y.: Doubleday and Co., Anchor Books, 1945.

C. S. Lewis. *The Screwtape Letters.* N.Y.: Macmillan Co., 1962.

Arthur Miller. *The Crucible.* N. Y.: Viking Press, 1959.

—— *The Death of a Salesman.* N.Y.: Viking Press, 1949.

Henry Miller. *The Tropic of Cancer.* N.Y.: Grove Press, 1962.

—— *The Tropic of Capricorn.* N.Y.: Grove Press, 1961.

*John Middleton Murry. *Things to Come.* N.Y.: Macmillan Co., 1928.

*Lewis Mumford. *The Conduct of Life.* N.Y.: Harcourt Brace, 1951.

*—— *In the Name of Sanity.* N.Y.: Harcourt Brace, 1954.

Walker Percy. *The Moviegoer.* N.Y.: Popular Library, 1962.

*Elmer Rice. *The Adding Machine.* N.Y.: Samuel French, 1923.

Jean-Paul Sartre. *Existential Psychoanalysis.* Chicago: Henry Regnery Co., 1962.

*——*What Is Literature?* N.Y.: Philosophical Library, 1949.

*Oswald Spengler. *The Decline of the West.* Abridged ed. London: Allen and Unwin, 1961.

George Steiner. *Tolstoy or Dostoevsky.* N.Y.: Random House, 1959.

Henry Thoreau. *Walden.* N.Y.: Holt, Rinehart, and Winston, 1948.

Paul Tillich. *The Courage to Be.* New Haven, Connecticut: Yale University Press, 1959.

—— *The Religious Situation.* N.Y.: World Publishing Co., 1956.

Alexis de Tocqueville. *Democracy in America.* 2 vols. N.Y.: Schocken Books, Inc., 1961.

Leo Tolstoy. *What Is Art?* N.Y.: Liberal Arts Press, Bobbs-Merrill Inc., 1960.

Norbert Wiener. *The Human Use of Human Beings.* Garden City, N.Y.: Doubleday and Co., Anchor Books, 1954.